A COMPLETE GUIDE

TO TRADING PROFITS

By

Alexander Perry Paris

TRADERS PRESS, INC.
P. O. Box 10344
Greenville, S. C. 29603

Library of Congress Card Number: 75-84640
ISBN: 0-934380-05-8

Publications of Traders Press, Inc.:

Commodity Spreads: A Historical Chart Perspective
Commodity Spreads: Volume 2
Commodities: A Chart Anthology
The Trading Rule That Can Make You Rich *
Viewpoints of a Commodity Trader
Profitable Grain Trading
A Complete Guide To Trading Profits

A current catalogue of the above and many other trading-related publications and sample commodity charts may be obtained by writing Traders Press, Inc., P. O. Box 10344, Greenville, S. C. 29603.

To

Joanne

CONTENTS

OTHER WORK BY THE AUTHOR

THE COMING CREDIT COLLAPSE: An Update for the 1980's,
By Alexander P. Paris, Arlington House Publishing, 333 Post Road
West, Westport, CT 06880, 1980: $12.95

This best-selling book, originally published in 1974 and recently
updated, is a classic in economic and financial analysis. Alexander Paris
long ago correctly diagnosed the true underlying causes of our growing
economic and financial problems. The dozens of charts and tables clearly
demonstrate the long-term financial deterioriation and government
intervention that is the source of our troubles in recent years.

A knowledge of the credit trends and highly predictable credit cycles
described by Paris is indispensable to financial planning and investment
timing in today's volatile environment. Paris also explains what to look
for in the future and how to structure your investments and personal
finances to cope with it.

FREE MARKET PERSPECTIVES

Alexander Paris, a registered investment advisor and leading free
market economist, regularly applies his pioneering work on credit trends
and credit cycles to current economic and financial trends. *Free Market
Perspectives,* a monthly economic/investment newsletter, continuously
monitors the economy and financial markets within the context of the
credit cycle while also keeping sight of the long-term financial trends.
Paris also trains his unique credit-based free market economic analysis
on the problem of government interference with free markets—projecting
not only the resulting economic distortions but also the investment
opportunities that are created in the process.

Subscriptions: One year (12 issues) U.S. $65.00 (Add $15 for foreign
airmail delivery outside North America.) Address all inquiries to:
HMR Publishing Company, P.O. Box 471, Barrington, Illinois 60010.

FOREWORD

No financial game holds more attraction than the stock market, and no aspect of the stock market is more alluring than trading for short-term profits. Most traders, however, prepare themselves no better for this game than for that other famous game, Monopoly. Consequently, there are many more losers than winners. Their salvation might have been a sound knowledge of charting and technical analysis but, unfortunately, this much heralded art has caused many more losses than profits. There are several reasons for this paradox: first, most charting books clearly explain the theory of charting but do not take the necessary additional step of explaining how to gain the necessary charting experience without the loss of most of one's trading funds; secondly, this same literature usually encourages the reader to embrace the cult of charting to the exclusion of common sense and of any previous knowledge of investing which he might have gained in his earlier trading. It would have him completely ignore any underlying fundamental values of the security being traded.

This work explains the theory of charting; it also takes the important step of explaining how to work the newly acquired knowledge smoothly into a viable trading system that utilizes not only charts, but also considers all other helpful information. Even more important, the reader will be able to apply what he learns here with less risk than he is now assuming with his present method of short-term trading.

SECTION I

The Groundwork

Chapter 1
INTRODUCTION

One of the most commonly extolled virtues of common stock investing, that of liquidity, is unfortunately also the cause of most stock market problems and losses. The ease of assuming or liquidating security positions leads to frequent and often violent price fluctuations. It is these very fluctuations, with their promise of easy overnight profits, that attract new speculators from all walks of life to short-term trading like moths to a flame. Indeed, no activity has been the target of as much thought and study as the attempt to profit from these frequent price fluctuations.

Nor is this an idle pastime, for he who masters these elusive price swings has his financial success assured. Nowhere else are the prospects of reward faster or greater than in short-term trading. Unfortunately, wherever the prospects of reward are the highest, there also will be found the greatest risk. The stock market is no exception to the rule. It is in trading the small-price swings that the premium is the highest on skill and knowledge, and here the speculator will find his greatest challenge. It is also here that losses are the largest for, although the premium is on skill, the average speculator is most ill-equipped and ill-informed in this area. Although a small number of speculators have been extremely successful at trading, most have suffered losses.

Where does the difficulty lie, and why do so many traders, many of whom are probably very successful in other pursuits, fail so miserably in the stock market? Can anything concrete be done to improve their results appreciably? The answer is yes, but first let's look at the problem and analyze what most of them are doing wrong.

THE PROBLEM

One difficulty underlies the entire problem of short-term trading. This is the fact that the shorter the time-period of the price swing under study, the more indirect the relationship between the price fluctuations and the actual or prospective values of the firm represented by the security being traded. The price movements may, at times, be entirely unrelated to any intrinsic values of the stock. It is for this reason that an intelligent study of a firm will not always be helpful when trading its stock. This problem will be examined in depth later in this book. In the light of this problem, however, let us see just how most of the traders go wrong. Although there may be many reasons for each individual failure, it is possible to divide most failures into two broad categories.

THE DOOMED

The first category of traders is predestined to failure. Although the traders in this group are numerous, their expected lifespan in the market is short. Notwithstanding some minor victories from time to time, eventually they must lose. These traders, anxious to profit from short-term price swings, make little attempt to understand the reasons for stock price movements and make even fewer attempts to think for themselves. They trade on tips or rumors and look for others to make their decisions for them. One of the syndromes of a member of this not-so-elite group is a high propensity for switching from one stockbroker or securities firm to another. This type of trader is looking for the "magic" broker or firm that will miraculously transform his savings into a fortune. Usually, even if given good advice, he ignores it or sells out impatiently if a stock recommendation does not work out immediately.

There is nothing that can be done for this type of trader. He will continue to drift until either his savings are gone or he finally realizes that, as a first step to success, he must be willing to think for himself and work toward understanding the forces that control stock price movements in the short term.

THE CURABLES

The traders in the second category, for whom this book is intended, are those who can be helped. They are willing to work and intelligently attempt to find the key to trading.

4

They want to learn to make their own decisions and are trying to discover the reasons behind short-term price fluctuations. Their problem is that no approach to the stock market can be completely scientific in nature and, in the area of short-term trading, it is most difficult to systematize an approach. In their search for a final solution, these traders separate themselves into two schools of thought, each of which makes one basic blunder which keeps success just beyond its reach.

The Fundamentalists

This first group may be said to practice the *fundamental* approach to stock market analysis, which has a very specific meaning in stock market parlance. In this case the target of the analysis is the *firm* itself, and the price fluctuations and market action of its common stock are only incidental. If the analysis and prediction of future success of the firm are correct, the price of its common stock should reflect its success, and the speculator should be rewarded by profits. This is certainly true as far as it goes. The success of any firm, *in the long run*, depends upon its ability to earn increasingly greater profits. The analytic approach that can accurately predict future profits will certainly not go unrewarded. And the fundamental approach does have as its goal the prediction of future profits. The traders in this group will approach their goal through a study of the firm's financial statements, its products, its management, industry trends and the condition of the entire economy.

All of these factors are classified as the firm's "fundamentals." They are all important in determining the long-run trend in profits. Of course, the basic error made by this group, apart from any inadequacies in fundamental analysis, is that they are attempting to use these fundamentals to make short-term trading decisions and, as mentioned earlier, the shorter the time period under study the less direct the relationship between the fundamental values of a company and the price fluctuations of its stock.

The Technicians

The second group of traders has taken a further step in the

5

right direction and can be considered to be further advanced than the *fundamentalists.* They belong to the technical school. The traders in this category are wise enough or experienced enough to realize that there are important causal factors in short-term price swings that cannot be predicted by fundamental analysis of the firm. Analysis of these factors is called *technical analysis* and, although it will be explained in depth later, a brief explanation will be helpful at this point.

Just as the price of a stock responds to news of a fundamental nature as discussed above, there are many price fluctuations in individual stocks or in the market as a whole whose origin cannot be traced to any specific news of the firm itself. The fluctuations are instead caused by conditions or forces in the market itself. A few examples should make this clear: Consider the stock that has risen very rapidly over a period of time with no rest or "profit-taking." This stock is termed by the technician to be "overbought." That is, there are too many short-term traders who have quick profits in the stock that have not been taken. Sooner or later some shock will send these traders suddenly scurrying for their profits, causing a *technical* or profit-taking sell-off. The stock was technically vulnerable to a sell-off and, the longer it was put off, the steeper the technical decline. A similar problem is encountered when too many short-sellers take positions in a stock. Sooner or later, the high short interest will cause a *short-covering* rally. Again, a technical cause of short-term market action.

In each example above, the condition of the firm or its earnings, dividends, sales, or other fundamental considerations do not explain the decline or the rally. The fluctuations were strictly technical phenomena. There are literally hundreds of such technical considerations or situations that have a great influence on short-term fluctuations. In fact, as we shall see, over the very short term, these are the considerations that are most influential in price fluctuations.

There are, of course, numerous attempts by many traders to systematize the technical influences upon price fluctuations. Many of the *systems* are sophisticated enough to get into print in books or in newsletters from advisory services; unfortunately, they are taken as gospel by many of the tech-

6

nicians. The systems may, for example, be based upon volume of trading, odd-lot transactions, short sales, odd-lot short sales, money market figures or upon many other freely available data. The problem arises when one of these systems is taken by traders as a complete answer in itself to the riddle of short-term price fluctuations. This is, of course, the first major blunder committed by this technical group. They drift from one system to another, expecting each one to be the magic key to profits. A few losses and discouragements later, a new system is sought. Each experiment is costly, and the average trader either runs out of money before he runs out of systems or he becomes an avowed long-term investor.

The sad truth is that most of the technical tools have at least a grain of wisdom in them, or they would not have become popular. The same may be said of many old and familiar market sayings that have endured over the years, such as "sell on good news" or "buy on bad news." They have been nurtured out of experience, much of which was costly to someone. Each cannot, however, be taken and applied in the absence of any other consideration. The average speculator does not profit from *his* mistakes if he merely tries each tool unsuccessfully and then abandons it in disgust to move on to another. If he would, instead, squeeze the grain of wisdom from each and combine them into one working system of trading, he would have the system he so anxiously seeks. He would then be profiting from the accumulated wisdom that has been passed on through years of experience. A beginning toward such a system, and the most important topic of this book, is the system of charting.

CHARTING AS AN ANSWER

Charting is the most widely accepted system of technical analysis. It is an organized attempt to bring many of the important technical concepts into one trading system aimed at forecasting stock prices over the short term. A system that has gradually expanded over the years, it is practiced today by thousands of traders around the world. It is not only an extremely helpful tool but a necessity to the short-term trader. Indeed, any attempt to trade the market without this type of aid will surely end in failure. This system will be examined in detail later but, first, let's examine some of its problems.

In spite of the wide acceptance of charting by major brokerage firms and other financial institutions, there is probably more money lost by the average speculator through charting than by any other method of trading. This should not be the case for, if properly used, charting is a valuable weapon for short-term trading.

One of the major problems is that most of the pundits of charting all follow the same hard line. The speculator, according to charting lore, must be in one camp or the other. He must be either the pure chartist who ignores all fundamental factors including common sense, or he must be a pure fundamentalist. He is not allowed to work with both as he masters the basic principles. The average beginning chartist, who has probably already lost money trading, is anxious to try out the new system as soon as he has finished a basic text on the subject. He abandons completely whatever he has learned up to that point and goes enthusiastically into battle with his newly acquired armor. After several discouraging losses, he usually quits in disgust long before he has learned the true potential of charting. The art of charting will be learned only through experience on the firing line.

Contributing to this problem is the preponderance of charting texts that do little more than explain the basic theory and principles of charting. They stop one step too soon in their treatment. They offer no bridge between theory and practice. They offer no detailed plan for gradually working the new tool into the daily trading practice of the speculator to help him avoid many of the losses due to inexperience. Nor do they show how the speculator may use much of the previous fundamental knowledge he has acquired to help cushion the changeover.

PURPOSE OF THE BOOK

The purpose of this book is: first, to convince the reader of the need for technical analysis in short-term trading; second, to acquaint him with the most important basic principles of technical analysis; and, finally, to show him how to work this new system smoothly into the fundamental approach he has probably been using, and ultimately to blend both together into a workable and viable system of short-term trading which will prepare him for any trading situation.

Because charting is one of the basic foundations of a good trading system, a large portion of this book will be devoted to an explanation of the techniques of charting. The reader will not find, however, many of the intimate details of construction and analysis found in many texts, for it is not the aim here to create more "charting monsters," but more successful traders. The aim is, instead, to instill in the reader the basic concepts of charting and then, more importantly, to show how they may be used in an overall system of trading.

But perhaps a "charting monster" should be defined: he is the person who goes overboard. It is very easy to be deceived by the seemingly scientific nature of charting and to expect too much in the way of scientific consistency. There are, for example, many elaborate systems utilizing semi-logarithmic paper, moving average lines superimposed upon impressive charts, and all seeming ultra-scientific. The failing is, of course, that the profit performance does not usually match the attractive appearance of the charts. In this book, the most simple system of charting will be used, a system that will demonstrate and not bury the basic underlying concepts of charting.

CHARTS ARE NOT THE COMPLETE ANSWER

I stress the importance of avoiding an overemphasis on charts because, unlike most chartists, I feel that charts serve their best purpose when used in conjunction with good fundamental analysis and common sense. Just as the short-term trader will find trading impossible without the use of technical aids, he will be equally handicapped if he attempts to ignore fundamentals completely. It is equally important to develop both skills. Although space does not permit a complete exposition in this book of the fundamental approach, it is assumed that the reader already has some fundamental knowledge of the market either through reading or experience; otherwise, he should study the fundamental approach in conjunction with this reading.

As any temperamental French chef will agree, it is not the

ingredients alone that make the dish a success, but the way that they are blended by his skillful hands. The same should apply to trading. Knowledge is, of course, important but more important still is the way that it is used. There are many knowledgeable traders who never make a dime, for they are lacking one important ingredient. In this book we will attempt to outline all of the most important ingredients for success and to blend them into a workable system that neither underutilizes nor overrates any individual tool.

We shall begin with a brief discussion of the theory of charting and its most important basic concepts. Next, we shall discuss the important mechanics of chart construction, short sales and stop orders in preparation for the discussions that follow. Then, the analysis of charts will follow. Here the reader will learn to recognize the important signals given by charts in the form of recognizable chart pictures and volume characteristics. In the third section of the book, the reader will then begin to see how his newly found skills can be blended smoothly into his previous trading system. He will find that, unlike most beginning chartists, he can begin to profit from charting immediately, while suffering a *fewer* number of losses rather than *more* while he is still learning his technical lessons. We shall start with a simple system combining both charting and fundamental analysis, but with greater emphasis upon the fundamental.

Then, the charting portion of the system will be gradually refined and emphasized. Finally, after we have arrived at the fully refined trading system, we will add the final ingredient to success—the proper trading psychology. The final product should be a complete system of trading which will fit every occasion, can gradually be improved, and will return consistent profits.

Chapter 2

THE THEORY OF CHARTING

The concept of making trading decisions based upon anything but fundamentals is no doubt quite new to many readers. Before we plunge into the details of building an organized trading plan based upon a solid foundation of charting procedures, it will be helpful to look first at the broad concepts of technical analysis. We shall look not only at the benefits of each of the two broad approaches but also at their shortcomings.

INADEQUACIES OF A PURELY FUNDAMENTAL SYSTEM OF TRADING

An easy way to appreciate the necessity for technical analysis in a short-term trading scheme is to picture a system of trading that utilizes only fundamental analysis. From our brief encounter with fundamentals in the first chapter, we know that fundamental analysis deals with the investigation of the *firm*. The information needed for decision-making is familiar to anyone who has done any investing at all: earnings per share, sales, asset values, profit margins, return on equity, etc. The list of necessary financial data is almost endless. Other news, such as stock splits, management changes, new products, competition, patents, and other fundamentals of a qualitative nature, are also pertinent. Ideally, the analyst will include, in his study, *all* of the important data which may have any bearing upon the future success of the firm. There are several excellent texts on security analysis that offer systematic approaches to gaining this end. Theoretically, if the reader were to follow any of these systems religiously, he would have a good record in predicting future profit trends of the firms he investigates. In the long run, it is the earnings per share that determine the value of any equity security. Even the most avid chartist will admit this proposition. For long-term investing then, there is little need to consider charting except, as we shall see, to aid in taking the long-term

11

position at the best possible price. The question is, however, how well this method of analysis suits the needs of the trader interested only in the short-term fluctuation of the stock, and not in the long-term growth or in the safety of stock as a long-term investment.

The first general inadequacy of the purely fundamental approach has to do with the sheer bulk of information necessary to make an intelligent decision. Security analysis is certainly a well-organized approach, but most investors do not have the time, patience or ability to consider all relevant factors. Even the long-term investor, using this approach, is bound to leave out some important factor in his analysis most of the time. The short-term trader, always interested in a new stock to trade, is even less capable of making a complete and accurate investigation.

A second inadequacy deals with the availability of the information. Even the trader or investor who has the necessary ability and patience to consider all relevant factors will find that he is unable to find all of the information necessary to reach a decision on each factor. How often, for example, would the average analyst be able to find the information necessary to decide on the validity of a patent covering an important product of the firm under study? In addition, there is another aspect of information availability that more directly affects the short-term trader. The average trader must glean his vital financial information from the firm's accounting statements which are available to him, at best, only once every three months. Some companies report the all-important earnings per share and sales performance data only twice per year. Dividend meetings, where changes in dividend payments, large stock dividends, stock splits, and other information is often divulged, are held quarterly also. Relatively infrequently, firms may announce mergers, new products, new contracts and other pertinent data. But what is the poor fundamental trader to do between news announcements? If stock prices reacted perfectly to news of fundamental changes, and if fundamental changes were the sole determinants of price fluctuations, such a problem would not exist. Prices would remain relatively stable between news announcements, and then would react either up or down solely in response to news. But we know this is not the case. Instead, the stock market is constantly fluctuating, quite wildly at times. Very often, there is a total absence of any news at all pertaining directly to a stock which is experiencing a steep rise or decline in price. By the time that the reason for the movement is discovered, if ever, the short-term trader may have already suffered a sizable loss. Unfortunately, the short-term trader has little choice but to trade on the news as he receives it and to act blindly between news announcements. As we will see below, even when he receives the actual fundamental news regarding the firm it will, as often as not, lead him to make the wrong short-term trading decision, since the news had been discounted in varying degrees.

The third inadequacy of a purely fundamental trading system is based upon this phenomenon of discounted news. We have seen that the average trader is forced to rely upon news announcements in his trading but, because of discounting, he is almost always at a disadvantage.

Discounted news, simply defined, is news that has already had its impact upon stock prices. That is, any action that would be taken in response to the news, in the form of either a purchase or sell order, has already been taken, and the price of the stock already reflects the effects of the news even before it has been announced. This is because the officers of the firm, their relatives, their friends, friends-of-friends, key employees, and many others who learn of the news act upon it well before it is made public. In addition to this "insider" buying or selling, there is also action taken on rumors of the news and on the advice of a few shrewd analysts who guess at the content of the news announcement. Very often, the price rise is much greater than the news actually warrants and the stock has already moved too far without any profit-taking. When the news announcement is finally made, and the unfortunate fundamental trader makes his purchase on the strength of what he considers to be good news, he is immediately rewarded with a short-term loss as earlier buyers take profits on the news.

Even when the more knowledgeable fundamental trader is aware of the phenomenon of discounting, he is still faced with the difficult question of the degree to which the news has been discounted. The type of price reaction to such news is not an isolated situation, but one that may be expected to be the rule. So consistent is this action that it has given rise to two market sayings that have persisted for many years: "Buy on the bad news," and "Sell on good news." Nor is discounting due only to the actions of the chosen "insiders" of the firm. Future events, known to all in the market, are most often discounted well before the event actually occurs.

For example, as this book is being written, the market is awaiting the passage of a federal tax surcharge which will supposedly cure many of the economic ills facing the nation. From the moment that it became almost certain that the tax package would pass, the market began to rise as the market looked ahead to its passage; i.e., it discounted its passage. When the tax was actually approved, the market, instead of rallying on the bullish news, quite predictably began to decline. The traders, no longer having the good news to look forward to, took their profits. They mentioned instead the immediately bearish effects of the tax, such as lower corporate earnings, less spending power by the public and other deflationary effects. Now they had bearish news to discount. Once again, the difficulty of trading the fundamentals is demonstrated.

In addition to the difficulties mentioned above, it must be remembered that there are a myriad of price-making determinants that have nothing to do with the fundamentals of the firm. None of the millions of traders and investors in the market has a complete and accurate appraisal of the company in which he is trading. He may be buying or selling on erroneous fundamentals, on rumors or guesses as to future news, or simply according to his mood. Add to this the unreasonable fears and panics in times of war scares and other calamities, and their effects upon stock prices, and the trader may soon begin to wonder whether fundamentals are really studied, after all.

Finally, the trader can always count on the fact that everything in the market will be overdone. That is, when the stock is rising, overenthusiasm will always push it higher than either the fundamentals warrant or the analyst might reasonably expect. When stocks are falling, pessimism prevails and they decline far below what is called for by a realistic appraisal of the fundamentals. How can the trader, using only fundamental analysis, trade the stock once it has gone beyond the limits called for by its fundamentals? Yet, some of the most rewarding short-term trades occur in this area, when most fundamentalists would be out of their positions. This is one more important inadequacy of the fundamental approach.

Thus, we have seen that, while in the long run, prices are determined generally by the fundamentals of the firm and particularly by its earnings per share, there are a considerable number of barriers to the use of fundamental analysis for short-term trading. Although a number of inadequacies were mentioned, they may all be grouped into one major problem, that of *timing*. Fundamental analysis, properly done, will only tell the trader what is a good stock and what is a bad stock, what a stock *ought* to do in the market. It will not tell him *when* the movement will occur, especially in the short term. Nor does the fundamental approach consider the existence of other price-determining factors besides those considered in security analysis. It will not even tell the trader where to place stop-loss orders if he wishes to use them in his trading. The short-term trader obviously needs more help. That aid is technical analysis.

WHAT IS TECHNICAL ANALYSIS?

We have already had a brief introduction to technical analysis in the first chapter. Here, we will attempt to make the concept somewhat clearer. First, what is meant by the word "technical" when referring to a "technical rally," a "technical sell-off," or "technical strength or weakness," or to many other market phenomena? It is often said, tongue in cheek, that any price movement that the experts can't explain is termed technical. While this certainly points up that the term is overused and abused, it also, once again, indicates the great number of price fluctuations that cannot be explained by fundamentals. "Technical" factors are any determinants of price movements, that are not caused by any fundamental news regarding a firm. They are, more or less, self-determined by the market action of the stock.

15

Technical Analysis, then, unlike fundamental analysis, is *stock-oriented* rather than *firm-oriented.* It ignores the question of underlying values of the firm and concentrates entirely upon the market price of the stock as the only important value. So far, this sounds quite sensible, for the short-term trader's profits are certainly determined by the market prices at which he buys and sells, and not by some vague long-term underlying value notion. The analysis is aimed at assessing the technical strength or weaknesses of the stock to determine the possible short-term direction of the price.

Of course, it is difficult to pigeonhole everything into either the technical or the fundamental category. An example is the number of shares outstanding and available for trading in any firm. A firm with a very small number of shares outstanding will certainly react more violently in price to a sudden rush of demand or supply than a firm more generously endowed with shares. The number of shares outstanding can certainly be classified as a fundamental fact. On the other hand, the everyday trading in the stock may cause changes in the way the stock is distributed among the shareholders, which may in turn have changing effects on the market action of the stock. If, for example, the stock becomes popular with large institutional long-term investors or if officers of the firm decide to increase their positions for control purposes, the "floating supply," i.e., the shares available for everyday trading, may become quite "thin." The stock may then, temporarily, exhibit much more violent fluctuations than before. Later, it may change again as large positions are liquidated. A study of the shares currently truly available for short-term trading is an excellent example of technical analysis. There are, of course, many other aspects of technical analysis.

The true technician, however, goes much further than merely analyzing the technical aspects of price fluctuations. He feels that the market provides a complete trading system. It is assumed that all fundamental factors, fears, enthusiasms, pessimisms, and other emotions find their way into the market via a buy or sell order. All business news is immaterial since it has already been considered, chewed up, digested and spit out as an order. There are no secrets from the technician,

16

for everything is in the picture of the market action of the stock. It is only necessary to study the price and volume action of the stock and to learn how to read the signals that it gives.

Through technical analysis, many of the inadequacies of the purely fundamental approach are erased, and the unmanageable number of fundamental considerations are boiled down quite simply to the market price. The difficulty of gathering the necessary information in fundamental analysis is not present in the technical approach. All information, such as the price range, number of shares traded, short-interest, is freely available to all. The trick is to analyze it correctly. Discounted news is certainly no problem since business news is not even considered. Its effect upon the market price, however, is studied. Finally, as we shall see in our discussion of charting, timing of purchases and sales as well as the proper placement of stop-loss orders is very definitely improved through technical analysis. The only deficiency is that all of the important technical influences have not been brought together into one well-organized system of analysis. The closest attempt to such an organized approach is the system of charting which we shall now consider.

WHAT IS CHARTING?

The technique of charting is really quite simple. It is merely technical analysis and tape-reading put on paper. The price history, along with the volume of trading, is charted on graph paper on a daily, weekly or monthly basis. There are as many different charts and variations as there are chartists, but most systems contain this same important information. Some of the systems are quite elaborate, for there is something about graph paper that affects some people in strange ways. It seems to give a pseudo-scientific credence to charting that should not really be there, and many chartists become so lost in the elaborateness of their system that they forget the primary purpose—profits. As the reader will discover, I prefer the very minimum of complexity and look upon charting only as a very important aid to trading. It is quite easy to lose track of the truly significant technical concepts when the system becomes too complex.

Armed with charts of stock price and volume history, the chartist has all that he needs for his short-term trading. He knows how many shares are being traded and he knows the market price. He does not want any other facts that might confuse him. The market price represents, you will recall, the evaluation of all interested parties of all the fundamentals of the stock and of all other important factors, both of a reasonable and of an unreasonable nature.

Actually, his analysis of the charts is no more than a study of the demand for, and supply of, the stock at any given time. He is studying the charts to discover any *significant* changes in the balance between supply and demand. This change in the balance may show up in either or both of two ways: his first clue may be a significant change in the volume characteristics of the stock. The pattern that the price action forms on his chart will give him a second clue. Usually, either the buyers or the sellers are in control of the stock. The trend of the stock price would then be in the direction of the side in control. If neither side clearly has the upper hand, the stock will usually falter in a sideways movement with no clear trend. The chartist would then be on the lookout for the first change that would indicate the start of a new trend.

As for the price patterns, there are many that have been found, over the years, to occur over and over again in the same shape. The shape of these patterns and the type of price movement that usually follows have been observed to be so consistent that they have predictive value for the experienced chartist. We shall study the more important and consistent of these patterns in the next section.

One of the important claims of charting can be quite useful to the short-term trader. Charting takes some of the confusion out of discounted news. The fundamental trader, as we saw, is usually the last one to get in or out on most news. The chartist claims that he can improve the lot of the trader by at least one step. The insider is, of course, the first to take his position in the stock. As the insider buying progresses, however, it must eventually appear somewhere on the chart as a shift in the supply-and-demand picture, if the chartist is sufficiently skilled to discover it. The effects of a pending news announcement will often be displayed on the chart long before the public learns of it. The chartist, while still not as well off as the insider, can at least be one step ahead of the fundamental trader, who is waiting for the news before he acts.

The other important and quite valid claim of the chartist is that timing is immediately improved by the use of charts even if used in conjunction with fundamental analysis. Charts don't tell you which stocks are good and sound or which *should* move, but instead tell you which stocks are moving, which ones will move, and how far they are likely to move in the short term. This is, of course, what the trader really wants to know. Fundamental analysis will give the analyst any number of stocks that *should* move but only technical analysis will tell him *when* they will move.

This points up many of the frustrations that plague the fundamental trader. He may, for example, perform a thorough and accurate fundamental analysis of his stock and see his judgement vindicated quarter after quarter, as the earnings rise as expected but, alas, with no price move whatsoever. Finally, when he liquidates his position out of boredom, the stage is set for the big move, naturally without our analyst. Even the best analysts who ferret out the most interesting of special situations often sell out too soon through boredom or a lack of conviction, only to see the stock move later. The chartist, on the other hand, believes that, no matter how interesting the stock, it should only be interesting to the short-term trader when it is beginning to make its move. The chart, hopefully, will signal the beginning.

There are also a number of more obvious advantages using charts as helpful trading aids. As we shall see, the chart offers many logical and helpful points for the proper placement of protective stop orders. In fact, stop orders are almost entirely useless without the aid of charts.

Finally, even one uninitiated in the theory of chart analysis can gain a great amount of useful information from a brief study of a stock chart. He can acquire an instant acquaintance with the trading behavior of the particular stock under study. At a glance, he can see if the stock usually has wide

daily ranges or, instead, a characteristically dull price behavior unsuited for trading. Also available is a record of the
usual trading volume.

A WORD OF CAUTION

After extolling the merits of charting, it is only fair, before
concluding this chapter, to expand upon my earlier statement
that more money is lost through charting than is gained. Most
charting texts, needless to say, do not mention this. Indeed,
it is the purpose of this book to not only impress upon the
aspiring trader the need for technical analysis but also to
warn him of the dangers of its improper use.

The highest mortality rate for chartists is, not surprisingly,
among beginners. Some of the reasons I have already mentioned briefly. It seems that most casualties fall into either of
two extremes: The first does not take charting too seriously,
does not study it too carefully, but decides to dabble in a
little technical trading, most of which understandably ends in
disaster. The second embraces charting too enthusiastically
and expects too much of the sudden key to riches that he has
found. Though he studies much harder, his results are often
just as disastrous. Let's see how their troubles develop.

Because the charting principles seem quite simple on the
surface, the average beginning chartist feels he is ready to
begin profiting from his new tool immediately following a
cursory reading of a text. He is ready to take a position at the
first sign of any pattern that may even remotely resemble one
of those explained in this text. Worse yet, he completely and
immediately abandons any knowledge of fundamental analysis he might have learned previously. He will buy a stock that,
before his introduction to charting, he would not have
dreamed of buying after only a perfunctory analysis of its
fundamentals. Where previously he might have spent hours
analyzing the stock from a fundamental standpoint, he is
prepared to take a position after a quick glance at the chart.
Obviously, no system of trading can be this miraculous.
Nevertheless, this is a very common reaction of the beginning
chartist. And most charting texts written to date do very
little to discourage this reaction.

Even worse is the common technical indoctrination that
fundamental information cannot be used in conjunction with

20

charting. This, of course, encourages the beginning chartist to jump into the water immediately, with no protection other than his recently learned and still hazy technical concepts. The texts give no advice about starting slowly, relying heavily at first on sound fundamentals. This would run against the grain of the pure chartist.

The end result of all this is quite obvious. Most new chartists suffer a few substantial initial losses, drop charting before they ever really learn it, and look for some other magic system. The shame is that charting was probably the system they were looking for.

Another reason for frequent losses by beginning chartists and even by those who last long enough to be considered experienced, is psychological in nature. The chart gives not only buy signals but also sell signals. The beginner is always very quick to follow a buy signal and take his position solely on the basis of technical analysis. He will seldom, however, follow the same chart when it gives him a signal that he has made a mistake and should liquidate and take his loss. He then feels that his stock is immune to technical weakness and begins to look for fundamental reasons why his position should be held instead of liquidated for a loss. He therefore defeats the purpose of charting. Even here, though, a case might be made for holding on to avoid the loss if the long-range fundamental outlook for the stock is bright. Very often, however, chart trading takes the trader into issues fundamentally very weak, since the cult of charting allows no consideration of fundamentals.

Most of the shortcomings of charting can be overcome with a little common sense and the realization by the reader that, regardless of the attractiveness of charting, he is not relieved of the burden of thinking by his new system. With these, charting can become a very important addition to and, indeed, the basic foundation of a successful trading system.

In this book, after a brief introduction to all of the major charting concepts, a complete section will be devoted to working the new information into a well-rounded trading system that avoids many of the pitfalls mentioned above. We will learn how to take the risk out of charting, and much of the poor timing out of fundamental analysis.

21

Chapter 3

THE BASIC TOOLS

The stock chart is the primary tool of the technical analyst and the object of most of his analysis. Before we can learn how to analyze the chart and apply it to trading, there are several more details to consider. In this chapter, we will discuss the actual construction of charts, the use of buy-and-sell stop orders, and the use of the short sale.

CONSTRUCTION OF CHARTS

As mentioned previously, there is a great variety of charting methods and construction, some of which tend to become quite eleborate. However, the chart used in this book, the simple bar chart, is more than adequate for any situation. It is the easiest chart to read and the most simple in construction. It does not take the attention away from the very basic concepts of charting. It is very easy, as mentioned, for many beginning chartists to become lost in the system and the niceties of construction, completely losing the basic theory of what is being done. In becoming embroiled in intricate schemes, they are putting their emphasis upon the details of construction rather than upon the more important *analysis*. It seems that the more details and frills that are used, the less need the chartist feels he has for common sense in his trading. After finishing this book, the reader may make up his own mind on how complicated he wants his charts. In figure 3-1, we have an example of a common bar chart.

All that is necessary to begin charting is ordinary graph paper, the daily financial pages and a sharp pencil. Nothing could be easier or more convenient. Regardless of how complicated many technicians make charting appear, these simple requirements will enable you to take full advantage of all the principles of good charting theory.

The first step in construction is to properly set up the coordinate axes of the chart. Along the vertical axis, a relevant price scale is plotted. By relevant I mean that a little

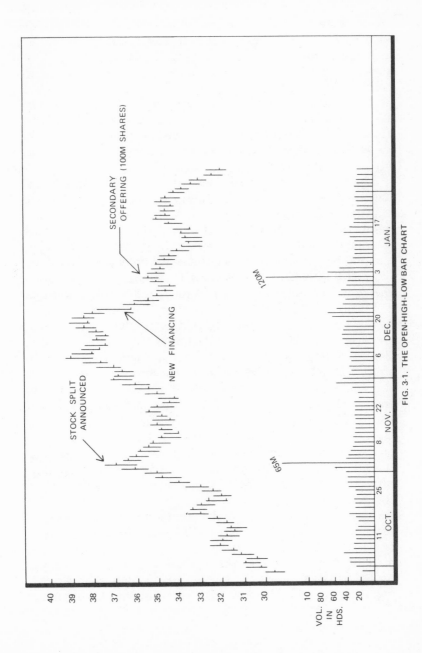

FIG. 3-1. THE OPEN-HIGH-LOW BAR CHART

effort at the beginning of each chart can save the chartist a lot of trouble later. The price scale should be set on each chart to match as closely as possible the price activity of the stock being charted. If the stock is a low-priced stock, each eighth of a point is important percentagewise, and therefore the price scale should be delineated in eighths so that they may be drawn into the chart. If, on the other hand, an extremely high-priced stock like IBM is charted, a different scale would be required. Since an eighth of a point is relatively meaningless on such a high-priced stock, the lowest fluctuation of the price scale may well be a full point. Stocks in between these two extremes may require minimum fluctuations of a quarter or a point, a half, etc.

The dates will be recorded along the horizontal axis. These dates will vary according to the type of chart that is being constructed. Information may be gathered and charted on a daily, weekly or monthly basis. Each type of chart has its own merits, but the most important to the short-term trader, and the one utilized in this book, is the daily chart. With the daily chart, then, the dates along the horizontal axis will be the actual market days, with Saturdays and Sundays omitted.

Finally, on the bottom of the page, a separate scale must be set up to record the daily trading volume of the stock. Once again, a little forward planning will avoid trouble later. Before setting up the volume scale it would be helpful to study a number of back issues of the financial pages to see the trading habits of the stock. If the stock customarily trades 25,000 shares, a scale like that in figure 3-1 would hardly be adequate. Instead, each notation in the scale may change by 10,000 shares rather than 2,000. To plot the chart otherwise would cause the volume plottings to interfere with the price fluctuations above. Even with proper planning, often the stock will exhibit extraordinary trading days when the volume would be much too high for the scale. In these situations, rather than draw the volume to scale and perhaps run into the price chart above, it is sufficient to draw a line for that day that represents an obvious high volume day and mark in the volume on the chart as in figure 3-1. As the reader will see later, it is the *relative* volume that is most important to chart theory and not the absolute amounts.

24

Therefore, it is not necessary to be able to read the exact daily volume directly from the chart. It is the significant *changes* in volume that the chartist is interested in and not the number of shares traded. We will have much more to say about volume in another chapter.

Now, we are ready to record the information on the chart. We need only two types of information from the daily financial page; the price range and the trading volume. The price range, consisting of the high, low, and closing prices for the day, is the first to be recorded. First, mark in the high and low price for the day and connect the two prices by a straight line. The closing price may then be indicated by a horizontal line. Then, for the same day, the trading volume may be recorded at the bottom of the page. At a glance, the chartist is then able to see the high price for the day, the low price, the closing price and the approximate number of shares traded.

As far as the minimum requirements are concerned this is all that is needed in the construction of daily bar charts. According to personal preference, the individual chartist may include other helpful information on the same chart. Special notation, for example, of important events may be helpful, especially when using a system combining both fundamental and technical analysis, as will be explained elsewhere in this book. In the first place, this is an excellent way for the aspiring short-term trader to learn how the market characteristically reacts to various types of news announcements. After sufficient use, this system will enable the chartist to become quite proficient at predicting the response of the market to any given news announcement. As will be discussed in a later chapter, certain types of news announcements may have a great influence on the interpretation of certain chart patterns.

CHART SERVICES

For those who would like to learn charting analysis but do not have the time to keep up a sufficient number of charts, there are a number of chart services available from which charts can be purchased on a regular basis. It is very helpful, however, to begin if possible to construct your own charts until you have the feel for charting. Later, daily, weekly, or monthly charts can then be purchased.

Some care should be exercised in deciding what type of charts to use. Daily charts are a necessity for the short-term trader, but they are much more expensive. The monthly chart is probably the least useful except for its historical value. There is certainly not enough detail in them to use exclusively for trading. The weekly chart may be used successfully by the trader who is more interested in longer-term trades for capital gains. A combination of the daily and the weekly chart is most useful. Very often, important errors can be committed by the chartist who fails to consult both. The daily chart, for example, might exhibit a very bullish pattern which might be only a small part of a much larger bearish pattern that would be evident only from a study of a longer-term weekly chart. The beginning chartist with limited funds might settle for constructing his own daily charts and subscribing to the less expensive weekly charts.

THE SHORT SALE

An important trading tool for any short-term speculator is the short sale. Because it will be mentioned often throughout the remainder of the book, it would be well to pause for a short explanation for those who are not familiar with it and for those by whom it is misunderstood.

DEFINITION

Let us begin by explaining that the trader who sells short is selling something that he does not own. He does so with the aim of profiting by a decline in the price of the stock that he sells. Anyone who has observed the vagaries of the market has probably noticed that stocks fall much faster and more sharply than they rise. It is nothing to see a gain that has taken years to accumulate erased in a matter of days. Obviously, then, the short-term trading possibilities should be very good. Nevertheless, the short sale, at best, is used very sparingly by the average trader.

The mechanics of the short sale are actually quite simple. The key is that the stock that is sold by the trader is borrowed and delivered to the buyer, for there is a buyer who is waiting for a certificate just as in a long sale. The trader is

26

left, after the short sale, with the proceeds from the sale and an obligation to repay some lender the amount of stock that was borrowed. If the trader is correct in his judgement and the price of the stock subsequently declines, he is able to purchase the stock at a lower price and return it to the lender. Since the trader sold the stock at a higher price than that which was required to repurchase it, he is left with a profit after paying for the stock. Although all of this sounds complicated, it is not. All of the work is done by the brokerage firm through which you deal, and it is not much more than back-office routine. Perhaps the diagram below will make the mechanics clearer:

```
SELL . . . 100 Shares of XYZ Corp. at $40  . . . $4000

   Margin Deposit at 70%  . . . . . . . . . . . . . .  2800
   Total Credit  . . . . . . . . . . . . . . . . . . . . . $6800

BUY . . . 100 Shares of XYZ Corp. at $25  . . . . 2500

   Remaining Credit  . . . . . . . . . . . . . . . . . . 4300
   Subtract Original Margin Deposit  . . . . . . . . 2800

PROFIT  . . . . . . . . . . . . . . . . . . . . . . . . . . $1500
```

The transaction above begins with an original short sale at $40 per share. The proceeds of this sale of $4000 (ignoring commissions and taxes) are turned over to the firm from which your broker borrows the stock which he, in turn, must deliver up to the buyer of your short sale. You, as the seller, must then put up the same margin that is required for purchases on margin (in this example, 70%). This is to insure that your broker will have the funds to repurchase the same stock at some future date in order to repay the loan of stock. Unlike the long-margin purchase, there are no interest charges for the short seller. Later, if you have made a wise short sale, you will be able to repurchase the stock ("cover your short") at a lower price (in this example, at $25). In the example above, after the short was covered, there was a profit remaining of $1500 excluding all taxes and commissions.

TRADING WITH THE SHORT SALE

Trading from the short side and selecting candidates for short sales represents little departure from the previous discussions, with the obvious exception that a decline rather than an advance is anticipated. Both technical and/or fundamental analysis may be utilized for selection and timing. Obviously, the short-sale candidate should have either weak fundamentals or a bearish chart picture.

There are, however, a few trading differences between the short sale and the regular sale. A short sale must be clearly marked as such when the order is placed with the broker and sent to the floor for execution. Once on the stock exchange floor, the short sale may be executed only on an "uptick," that is, the price at which it is sold must be higher than the last different sales price. This is not necessary on a regular sale. Finally, a regular sale will take precedence on the floor over the short sale in the trading crowd.

SPECIAL PROBLEMS OF THE SHORT SALE

There are a few problems encountered in selling short that the trader does not meet when trading from the long side. He cannot, for example, rectify a mistake by patiently waiting and hoping that the general strength of the economy or the long range upward trend of the stock market will eventually help him to break even. Both the remarkable strength of the U.S. economy and the continuing phenomenon of inflation work against the short seller in the long run. Even dividends work against the short seller, for any dividend that is paid while the trader is short must be repaid to the lender of the stock.

In spite of these special problems, however, the short sale can be a very useful and profitable tool. It is only necessary that the trader recognize the added risk and take precautionary steps to minimize the potential loss from a poor trade. An obvious and effective precaution is the wise use of protective stop-loss orders. As we will see, charts are made to order for logical placement of such protective stop orders. In addition to this precaution, there are a number of other helpful moves that can be taken to minimize the risks of trading from the short side of the market.

PRECAUTIONS

Although we shall discuss the strategy of short selling in several of the following chapters, there are a few general

28

precautions that may be mentioned here. One very important consideration in the selection of a short sale is the number of shares outstanding and available for trading in the stock under study . . . i.e., the floating supply. As we now know, the smaller the supply of stock available, the more volatile the price swings of the stock. Since declines, to begin with, are sharper than advances, the addition of a thin stock is often too much for the short seller to cope with. It is usually far better to short the stock whose price may be expected to suffer the gradual deterioration with few sharp rallies that allow the trader to follow his trade down with stop orders without being taken out.

There is also the problem of the "short squeeze." The short squeeze may develop when the number of shares that have been sold short represents a large proportion of the floating supply. This is, of course, most probable when the supply is small to begin with. As a larger and larger proportion of the floating supply of a stock is tied up in "short interest" (the total number of shares sold short but not yet covered), sooner or later, critical proportions are reached when the price swings of the stock begin to be drastically affected by short-covering. The rallies become accentuated, while each decline is tempered by profit-taking by the same short sellers. Both the rallies and the lack of a sharp decline, become a special problem to the short sale. It reaches proportions of the short squeeze when there is no longer stock readily available for lending and short covering is forced. Needless to say, much of this can be avoided if stocks with small floating supplies are eliminated from consideration for short selling.

A second factor to be considered in choosing the short sale is the dividend rate. As mentioned earlier, the short seller must make good to the lender any dividends on the stock in which he is short. Obviously, the high dividend-paying stock detracts considerably from the potential profits of the short sale unless the expected profit is sizable or the trade is expected to be extremely short term in nature. Particularly to be avoided is the slow-moving, high dividend-paying stock.

STOP ORDERS

The stop order is doubtless one of the most useful—and, at

the same time—the most abused and misused of all short-term trading tools. Probably, also, much more money is lost than is saved by using stop orders. Yet, once this tool is understood and utilized in the proper manner, it will make trading more effective and more profitable.

DEFINITION

Very simply, the stop order is a suspended market order. The *market order*, the most commonly used order, is one that is executed on the floor of the exchange or over-the-counter at the best prevailing price at the time the order is placed.

Here is one example of the usefulness of the stop order. Suppose that for some reason you have decided that at one particular price, should it be reached, you would want to sell out your holding immediately with a market order. If you were able to watch the ticker tape and if you didn't change your mind when the time came, when you saw that price reached you could immediately tell your broker to enter a sell order at the market. Since the average trader cannot watch the tape constantly, the stop order will accomplish the same goal, but more efficiently. A sell-stop order may be placed below the market price and left there on the specialist's book. As soon as the price marked on the order has been traded at or below, the specialist will immediately sell the stock at the market. Your order would be executed even faster than if you were watching the tape.

The same procedure may be used with a buy-stop order, which is placed above the prevailing market price of the stock. Your reasoning would be, in this case, that if the market price moves up to a certain price, you would like to buy at the market. The buy-stop order would then be a suspended market order to buy. It is very common to protect short sales with such a buy-stop order. Once the higher price is reached, your order becomes a market order to buy and is executed immediately. Like other orders, your stop order may be entered as a day order, open order, or as an order for any other specific time period. Many traders use the stop to protect their positions while they are on vacation or otherwise unable to follow the market closely. The stop order has many other uses, many of which will be discussed in the pages that follow.

THE STOP-LIMIT ORDER

A stop order may also serve as a suspended limit order where, when the price is reached, the order becomes an order to buy or sell at a specific price. Generally, this type of order is not recommended because, in most instances, it may defeat the purpose of the stop order. The problem arises when the stop order is touched off. Since the order becomes a regular limit order, the trader runs the risk that the market will sell through his limit price and his order will fail to be executed. If a sell-stop limit order is placed below the market at $50, for example, the trader may see one sale at exactly $50 with the next and succeeding sales below that price. Since the first sale touched off the stop order and the next was below the limit, the order would not be executed if the stock continued to fall.

PROBLEMS OF THE STOP ORDER

Why is such a potentially useful tool so disastrous for most users? The problem is simple enough. Where is the order to be placed? Like charting, the stop order is useful only if used properly. Most people use them in a way that makes the old saying, "a little knowledge is a dangerous thing," seem very meaningful. Stop orders are placed strictly at random, as if the stock will somehow magically reverse itself just short of the stop price and then go on to greater profits. Traders place the stop order to "limit their losses" but do not somehow expect to be "stopped out," and are, of course, disappointed and disillusioned when their stock moves on without them after they lose their position on a random fluctuation. Even worse, they will place a stop to limit their loss and then continue to cancel the order each time the stock falls near their stop price until, finally, they find that their loss has not been limited after all.

The stop order should, instead, be placed only at a significant price level. If the price of the stock, in the case of a sell-stop, falls below the stop price, it should be a signal that much more selling will follow. That is, the sell-stop should be

31

placed at such a point that, if the stock remains above that point, the uptrend of the stock is still intact, but if it is penetrated the trend has reversed itself and a substantial sell-off will follow. How are these magic points to be found? While there are no such "magic" points that will work unfailingly, stock charts will certainly aid in pinpointing such critical price levels quite consistently. In fact, there is no other tool available which will enable the trader to use the stop order more effectively. Without charts, the trader can only indiscriminately place his stop orders at levels that have no basis in logic.

The stop order is one more example of the habit many traders have of abandoning logical thinking when they believe they have a gimmick that will eliminate any need for logic. They take leave of their generally good sense when any type of system is involved. An excellent example is the investor who, after completing an exhaustive investigation into the long-range merits of a particular firm, decides that it is extremely attractive as a long-term investment. Then, after taking his position, he immediately places a stop order several points below the market. It should take only a moment's reflection to see the ludicrous combination of a long-term investment with a close-stop order. Yet, this is often done. Obviously, the stop order is useful only to the short-term trader.

We will, in our system of trading, utilize the stop order generously. For when charting is an integral part of the trading scheme, we will have logical points to place stop orders for most trades.

SECTION II

Chart Analysis

Chapter 4

GETTING THE MESSAGE

With the basic definitions and the details of chart construction in hand, it is time to examine charting theory in detail. The importance of any market tool rests not in the beauty of its construction, but in its usefulness to the trader in his quest for profits. What, then, can charts tell the interested reader, how can he read what the chart is telling him and how can he use this information for improved profits?

There are first a number of advantages to charting that are readily apparent even to the totally uninitiated. A brief examination of any chart can enable the trader to acquaint himself with the market behavior of a stock to a degree that, without charts, would take months of observation to duplicate. At once, the long-term price and volume history of the stock may be seen. The trading habits of the stock are also immediately revealed. If the stock has a sharply cyclical or seasonal pattern, the information cannot excape the chart. If the stock has a steady market following and heavy trading volume or has the habit of taking wide daily price swings, this too is revealed. For the trader on the verge of taking a position, a chart is invaluable in bringing him quickly up to date on the most recent market behavior of the stock. In the absence of a chart, this information can be duplicated only through months of observation before taking a position. To take a trading position without this information is to begin with a disadvantage.

Although these points are obvious they are, nevertheless, sufficient to justify the use of charts by all traders. But what of the most appealing claim of the chartist? Can charts, in fact, predict the future price trends and market behavior of stocks? This, of course, may be a little more difficult to see and certainly will require a more penetrating analysis of the charts. It is not, however, as difficult as most skeptics might think.

In this section, the precepts and theories of charting and

35

technical analysis will be clarified. The technical language of the chartist, which at first encounter is confusing, will begin to make sense. When the reader is in possession of all of the parts he will begin to see the logic of the entire system. Behind each theory and, indeed, the system of charting as a whole, there is a great deal of logic and common sense. The theory of charting is not something that has been only recently developed. It has, instead, slowly evolved over as many years as the organized markets have existed. Each year new theories are added to the existing body of knowledge. Any idea that has endured long enough to be included in the system of charting is well grounded in experience and common sense. This will be particularly evident in the following chapter.

Chapter 5
SUPPORT AND RESISTANCE

At first glance, a stock chart will probably appear to be simply a series of unrelated price fluctuations. After continued study, however, some semblance of order will soon appear. First, it will be seen that stocks neither move up nor down in a straight line. Instead, they stop to rest occasionally before continuing in the direction of their primary movement. As the stocks move sideways on the charts, it will appear exactly as if the stocks are resting. The price of each stock, instead of making forward progress, will trade within clearly defined limits. The volume of trading will also slacken considerably for the duration of the resting phase. While many stocks show no consistency in the frequency of these pauses, the regularity of the intervals between such pauses on many other stocks is remarkable.

The chartist calls such an area a "congestion area," which it truly is. It is an area of confusion, where neither the buyers nor the sellers have the upper hand. Temporarily, they have battled to a stand-off. Some of these congestion areas are more significant than others, but there are very good reasons for each of them. The explanation for these areas, like all charting phenomena, rests very firmly upon a foundation based on the actual behavior of individuals in the market.

If, for example, a stock has been rising with little pause for an extended period of time, those who made purchases early in the move become increasingly anxious to take profits. The congestion area begins to form when the profit-takers finally can wait no longer. Their selling is usually joined by short-sellers who have been watching the uninterrupted move. They are taking this slow-down as the first signs of a sell-off. The sellers are not alone, however; many other traders, aware of the strength of the stock, have been waiting for just such a small decline to purchase the stock. Still other traders who sold the stock short a little too early are also buying-in their shorts, since they are now able to cut down their losses

37

slightly. Temporarily, then, the battle between the two sides results in a series of rallies and declines until one side or the other gains the upper hand.

An examination of any chart will uncover a number of these congestion areas. Some of them represent only short pauses in the trend, while others depict a pitched battle that extends over a period of months. It is in the closer examination of each of these areas that the chartist will find the predictive powers of charts. Many of these congestion areas will take on recognizable shapes which give the experienced chartist valuable information about the future performance of the stock. Their shapes or patterns will be discussed in the chapters that follow. Each of the areas supply useful trading information, however, based upon the theory of *support* or *resistance*. At times, these congestion areas will supply support to the stock's movement while at other times, they will act as resistance. Each of these terms, the first in the new technical language to be learned, will be discussed in turn.

SUPPORT

Support, although a general word with a number of meanings, means only one thing to the chartist. A support area is an area on his chart where buying may be expected to enter the market in sufficient quantities to reverse a decline which reaches that area or, at least, stem the decline temporarily. This may become clearer upon examining the chart in figure 5-1. As the stock rises, it leaves a series of congestion areas behind. Each of these price areas will act as a source of support under any subsequent declines. Whenever sellers gain temporary control and interrupt the upward trend, they will be met by strong new buying as soon as the selling carries the stock down to one of these underlying congestion areas.

The reader will discover that there are very practical reasons for this expectation, based upon very human behavior in the marketplace. While each support area was being formed on the way up, there were quite naturally a large number of traders and investors who had dealings with the stock within the narrow range of trading. Some placed purchase or sell orders at limits that were not executed, while many others filled orders within the price range. When the stock finally

38

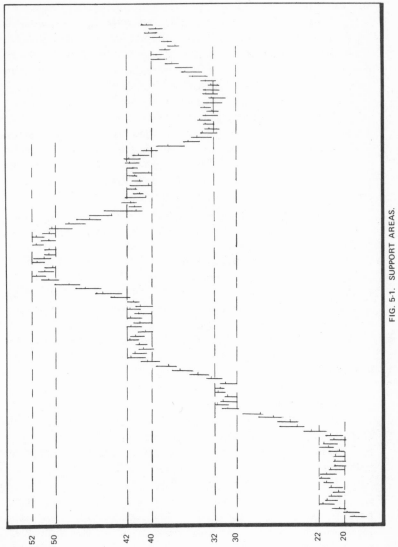

FIG. 5-1. SUPPORT AREAS.

broke out of the narrow confines of the pattern to continue its upward move, there were a number of mixed feelings. Those who made purchases and subsequently earned a nice profit are very happy to buy it again if the stock falls back to the same price area that they originally made their purchase. Many traders will trade the same stock over and over again if given the opportunity. Those who observed the stock or attempted to purchase it before the breakout but failed are angry at missing the subsequent move and will not make the same mistake if given another chance to buy.

Next, consider those who were the sellers in the support area. Needless to say, those who impatiently sold when the stock was moving sideways will be glad to rectify their error and replace their positions if the stock sells back to the point at which they liquidated. Finally, the short-sellers in the support area who have not yet taken their losses, will be happy to be able to break even and are eager buyers.

Put all of these people together and they make up a very powerful buying force waiting just below the market at the last congestion area, an area of support. In figure 5-1, our stock, after forming a congestion area with a top at $52, finally broke down to begin a decline. The chartist watching at that point would expect to find support first in the price area of $40—$42. The support at that range, although powerful enough to slow the decline, could not turn the tide. Finally, the support at $30—$32 was strong enough to reverse the decline. Had that area failed, further support remained at $20—$22.

The alert reader might, at this point, ask whether the buying evident in support areas is not present at all prices below the current market. The answer is, of course, yes. But the chartist is always looking for significant points on his charts, and in the price range of the congestion areas he knows that the buyers are concentrated enough to provide a meaningful support area. He can pinpoint their power by the fact that the stock traded for such a long while within the narrow price range. Though traders who had transactions in the long price moves *between* the support areas share the same feelings, there is not enough of them at any particular price range to pinpoint a meaningful support range.

During any decline, then, the chartist can confidently predict the price levels at which buyers will enter the market in significant numbers. Each congestion area left behind on the previous rise is a potential turning point for the decline. Some support areas are naturally stronger than others and, therefore, are more likely to be the areas at the ultimate bottom. Later, the reader will learn how to analyze each area in detail to assess their relative strengths.

RESISTANCE

Unfortunately, stocks do not always rise; they may, instead, decline over extended periods of time interrupted only by congestion areas similar to those formed while stocks rise. Usually, these congestion areas are formed at roughly the same price ranges of the support areas formed during the previous rise. You will recall from figure 5-1 how, as the stock declined, it paused at each support area until it was reversed. The buyers in each support area are enough to begin the sideways move. They, together with new buyers, form pockets of resistance that will hamper any future rally back up to that point. "Resistance," in this instance, refers to a price area where selling orders will enter the market in sufficient numbers to reverse the reasoning behind the theory of support to see the plausibility of resistance.

Each time the stock pauses at a previous support area on its downward path, all the potential buyers who comprise the support take their position, confident of another rise. They are joined by other buyers who witnessed the recent decline and decided that the stock looks like a bargain. Previous short-sellers also cover as the decline seems to falter.

When it finally turns out that the support area was not strong enough to contain the decline, and the stock resumes its decline, all of these new buyers are trapped with their long positions. Together, they represent one of the strongest and most consistent deterrents to rallies. Theirs is an attitude that is only too familiar in the stock market. They will hold on to their mistake until they can break even, no matter how long it takes. The longer and the further the stock falls, the more disgusted they become and the more likely they will be to just break even whenever the stock rises to their purchase

41

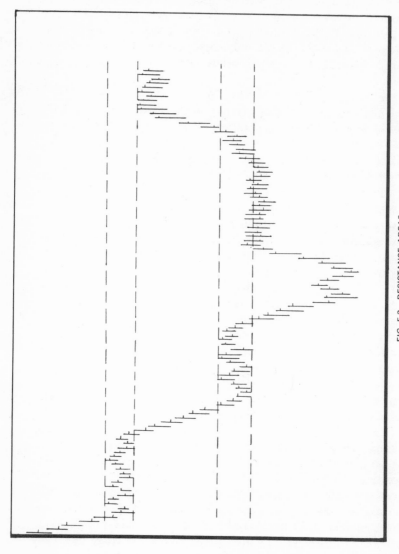

FIG. 5.2.   RESISTANCE AREAS.

price. Any rally back to this price area will be met with these angry sell orders which comprise the army of resistance. Each resistance area met during any subsequent rally will cause the rise to sputter and move sideways until, finally, one is strong enough to reverse the trend. And so it goes, as each long move retraces previous ground it always pauses at previous areas of support or resistance. It is especially the attitude of waiting to break even, however, that makes the theory of resistance even more reliable than that of support. Once again, although there are traders with losses at every price, it is only in the congestion areas where sufficient numbers of them can be pinpointed to give meaningful information to the chartist.

ANALYSIS OF SUPPORT AND RESISTANCE

It is not difficult to see the potential usefulness of this technique for short-term trading. Every extended price move in either direction is much the same. When the stock is retracing ground once covered in the past, the movement is one of fits and starts. The price will move very quickly between previous support or resistance areas and then slow down or reverse the move whenever one of these is encountered. Usually, there is only a sideways pause, but eventually one area will be powerful enough to reverse the trend. The possibilities of successful short-term trading between these areas are obvious and will be discussed, in detail, in later chapters.

When the price movement has taken the stock into new high ground, the problem of analysis becomes more complicated. Although the stock must still stop to rest periodically, it is much more difficult to determine just when the congestion area will occur, since there are no previous congestion areas to act as guidelines. The stock will simply rest whenever there are too many traders with short-term profits that must be taken. These periodic rests are very healthy for a stock and enable it to move much further later.

A dangerous situation is one in which a stock will not stop to take profits. Although this cannot be the cause of a sell-off in itself, when one finally comes it will be large and fast, since there is no support below the market. The trader who misses the first signals of weakness will suffer a costly lesson.

Most stocks, however, will stop periodically. Because no two support or resistance areas are of equal strength, the trader who is able to determine their relative effectiveness is well on the way to improving his trading profits. He will know which congestion areas are the harmless pauses in the trend and which are the powerful reversing areas.

1. VOLUME ANALYSIS

The key to the determination of relative strength among support and resistance areas lies in an analysis of the trading volume within the area. The more shares that change hands within the narrow price band, the more people are likely to be involved with the stock at those prices. The more people, in turn, that are involved in forming the support or resistance, the more effective it is likely to be. Therefore, the chartist should be very interested in the shares traded. It will tell him which area is most apt to turn the tide. With this information, his chances are excellent to buy a declining stock near the bottom of the move or to sell near the top.

As a rough estimate of the volume of trading, the length of the horizontal move on the chart is a good indication. The longest areas are most likely to contain the greatest volume. To be more accurate, however, a closer examination of the trading of each day is necessary. Not only can this analysis lead to an indication of the overall strength of the area but, as we shall see later, it enables the trader to pinpoint the most effective support or resistance price within the trading range. Any area or price of above ordinary volume is also potential support or resistance. Because there is always relatively high volume whenever a minor top or a minor bottom is made on the chart, it would be helpful to consider them separately.

As we have seen, each long-term price movement is composed of a series of minor rallies and declines, just as each congestion area is a collection of them within a defined price range. Minor tops are merely the highest points reached in each of these minor rallies, while the minor bottom is the lowest price in each trough. Because they characteristically exhibit high trading volume they constitute support or resistance in themselves. This is a very important point to remem-

44

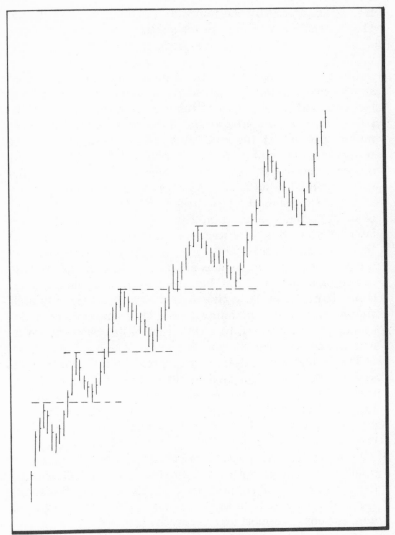

FIG. 5-3. MINOR TOP SUPPORT.

ber in the case of the fast-moving stock that seldom pauses long enough to build meaningful congestion areas. They, instead, experience periodic minor rallies or declines and then quickly resume their primary trend. Often the support or resistance offered by the minor tops and bottoms are all that the chartist has at his disposal for trading guides. Notice in figure 5-3 how each decline finds support at the previous peak.

Since each congestion area is comprised of a number of short-term price swings capped by such minor tops and bottoms, the major strength of the area is often exactly at the top of the support area at the line drawn connecting these minor tops or, in the case of a resistance area, at a line connecting the minor bottoms. They are the first line of defense. Because of this, a decline that reaches a support area will usually find its first support at the upper limits of the area without penetrating too deeply into the price range. This is an important trading hint that will be discussed in detail later. A move that is powerful enough to carry through this first line of defense deep into the support area should be watched very closely, as it is a good advance indication that the support area will not be strong enough to halt the decline. This is especially true if there was exceptionally high volume at most of the minor peaks. This same type of analysis applies equally well to a rally that has reached the lower limits of a resistance.

The second line of defense within the support or resistance area is often a little more difficult to find. Once a declining stock, for example, has penetrated the minor tops of the support area, there is usually one more significant support price within the area. This can be found only by examining the daily volume figures. If there are several outstanding volume days that took place at prices deep within the area, this smaller price range within the broader range might well be the most significant support price. If this point can be found, the trader may be able to save points by not waiting to sell until the entire support area is breached.

In short, the primary aim of volume analysis of support and resistance areas is to pinpoint the most specific and significant price within the support area as well as assessing the overall strength of the entire area. Once such a price can be isolated, a meaningful stop-loss order can be placed. If no such price can be found, the trader must wait for the final line of defense to be broken. This would be the bottom of the support area or the top of the resistance area.

As a final aid in pinpointing resistance, it is very helpful to keep a record of all large stock distributions and the price of the sale. They may be marked on the chart as indicated in Chapter 3. The sales price of such a large block is resistance in itself, and when found within a congestion area may be the most significant point within the area. Quite often there is a decline after such an offering, leaving a large number of buyers with a loss at one specific price and an overwhelming notion to break even once the stock rallies back.

2. NATURAL SUPPORT AND RESISTANCE

An often overlooked but helpful point of technical analysis is the tendency for traders and investors to set their sights on whole numbers. For example, a trader is more likely to give his broker an order to buy at $50 or $55 rather than at $50 1/4 or $55 1/8. For this reason there is always a great deluge of orders on the books of the specialist at such round numbers. There is, then, natural support or resistance at each whole number.

This knowledge can be very helpful in placing a stop order, for example, below a long position. If the trader has narrowed down the most significant support price to $50 1/2 and wishes to place his sell-stop just below that price, he would do better to place his sell-stop just below $50 to take advantage also of the natural support at that number. This would make his stop order even more meaningful. He is, in effect, giving his stock one more test before selling out.

The trader should, in fact, remember this point when placing any type of order and avoid the crowds at the whole numbers. If he wishes to sell at $40, for example, he should place his order instead at $39 7/8. Just as it is likely that a stock will finally top out at an important resistance area, it is also likely that it will be a whole number that will be the final top. By trying to sell at $40, the trader may miss out completely. On the other hand, if a purchase is desired at

$30, one should, instead, settle for $30 1/8 for similar reasons.

3. AGE OF THE AREA

Another important consideration in the analysis of the support or resistance area is its age. Certainly there must be a difference in the strength of a congestion area that is one month old and one that has aged for several years. It is difficult to answer this question correctly every time, since the answer rests upon the attitudes of traders who are trapped in an undesirable position. There are a few conclusions that can be made, however. First, to make resistance work, the trader must be suffering his loss long enough to become disgusted and ready to sell out to break even at the first opportunity. With this in mind, probably support or resistance that is less than one month old would not be too effective. That is, the buying or selling power in the area would probably not be great enough to delay the rally or decline to that point for very long, if at all.

On the other hand, areas that are older than one or two years begin to lose much of their effectiveness. After such a long period of time attitudes change, tax losses have been taken, and there is slow and gradual liquidation. A glance at many long-term charts will, nevertheless, still show many important areas that have held for many years. One old resistance area that is frequently effective after many years is the all-time high on a stock. Often, these highs are made with extremely high volume, accounting for the many traders who held out.

4. CHANGING SIDES

There is one more important point—already previously hinted at—to be made concerning support and resistance: a support that fails and is penetrated becomes a resistance area for any future rally. A resistance area similiarly breached becomes a support area for any future declines. Although this may be confusing at first, it is not too difficult. Recall that in figure 5-1, when each support area was reached in the decline, the buying that entered the market was enough to slow the decline temporarily. New buyers entered the market, helping to extend the sideways movement until the support was finally penetrated. A new congestion area was formed at the same price range as the older support area that slowed the decline in the first place. These disappointed buyers who formed the support that was not strong enough to hold are now the resistance on the next rally, in the same price range as the previous support. Thus, the same price range that offered the support, when penetrated, offers the resistance in the future. The stronger the support, the stronger resistance it will become if penetrated.

A FINAL NOTE

In this brief introduction to support and resistance, it should be obvious that this knowledge can be quite helpful to the average trader. In fact, many traders use a very simple system of charting based solely upon this theory and leave the more refined theories to the serious chartist. In the final section of this book the reader will be exposed to a similar system using both technical and fundamental concepts.

Although the discussion will now shift to more refined charting theories, this idea of support and resistance is basic to all other charting techniques. The reader will meet them again many times in these pages.

Chapter 6
TRENDLINES

After further close study of charts, the beginning chartist will make a second major discovery. Stock prices tend to move in a rather orderly manner, contrary to what one might believe after watching their daily gyrations in the financial pages or on the ticker tape. Once these fluctuations are put down on chart paper, they do not appear so aimless, and patterns begin to emerge. The chartist will find that a stock, once set into motion, tends to continue in that direction, with minor interruptions, until it finally reverses direction. The chartist terms this long directional move a "trend." It may be either an "uptrend" or a "downtrend."

The chartist—or any trader, for that matter—would like to take his position as close to the beginning of this trend as possible. He would then like to stay with the stock as long as possible, liquidating only when it appears that the trend has ended. Certainly, there can be no argument with this ideal goal. In the following chapters, the reader will be introduced to many methods that will help him accomplish this goal. The first step, however, is to be aware of the existence of the trend. Therefore, it is necessary to take a closer look first at the uptrend, and then at the downtrend.

THE UPTREND

DESCRIPTION

The most clearly discernible characteristic of the uptrend is the succession of higher tops and higher bottoms. As figure 6-1 shows, each minor top is higher than the previous one, and each minor bottom is also higher than any previous bottoms. A "trendline" may be constructed by drawing a straight line connecting all of the minor bottoms. Naturally, because each bottom is higher, the trendline will be slanting upward.

At least two minor bottoms are required to draw a trend-

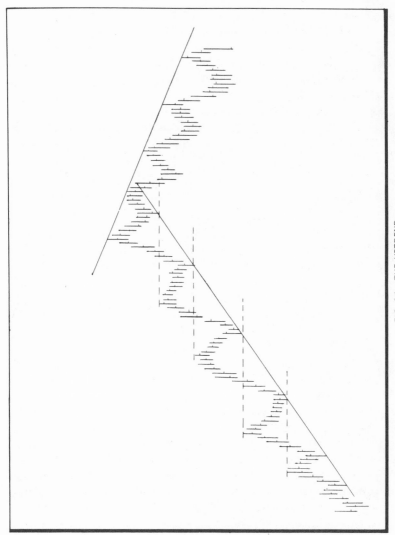

FIG. 6-1. THE UPTREND.

line. The chartist requires, as a minimum, not only two bottoms but also two minor tops with the second higher than the first. To understand the logical base to the trendline let us digress and discuss the trendline in terms of support and resistance.

Looking again at figure 6-1, which is admittedly a perfect chart, it can be seen that each minor top, once penetrated, becomes the support for any ensuing decline. Each minor bottom finds support in the vicinity of the previous top. The entire trendline, therefore, is a continuation of tests of support and resistance. Each penetration of the resistance of a minor top is a successful confirmation of the uptrend, and each minor bottom is also a successful test of the support of the previous top. The trendline connecting the minor bottoms acts as a line of support that continues to rise. Thus, each time the stock recedes to the trendline but does not penetrate it, is a successful test or confirmation of the trendline. For this reason, the chartist insists on the formation of the second top as a minimum effective trendline. It is a confirmation that the second bottom was, indeed, a true bottom. If this minimum trendline is extended upward, each succeeding minor bottom must be formed at or above this line. Each time the decline halts exactly at the extended trendline, the chartist grows more confident of the trendline.

TESTING FOR VALIDITY

Many chartists are not satisfied with only the minimum requirements of the trendline. Before they will use it for trading purposes they will ask a number of other questions. The conservative chartist insists on several other qualifications before he considers the trendline to be a valid one. A valid trendline is one that represents the true long-term trend of the stock and, when broken, would signal a reversal in the major direction of the stock. Although there are many minor points of trendline analysis, there are at least three major tests of reliability:

1. *Number of times tested*: Each time a minor decline finds its bottom on or very near to the trendline and then rallies past the previous top, a new successful test has been made. The more successful tests, the more valid is the trendline.

2. *Length of the line*: The longer the trendline, the more reliable it becomes. This is similar to the test above, except that it takes time into consideration. A series of tests that take place within a period of only several weeks is not as valid as one that takes place at greater time intervals. This is again tied back to the theory of support and resistance. A support or resistance area that is only a few days old is meaningless, and therefore a test of it is not meaningful as a test for the trendline.

3. *Angle of ascent*: The ideal slope of a trendline is about 45%. The trendline becomes increasingly unreliable as the slope steepens. The steeper the line, the greater the likelihood that chance sideways fluctuations may penetrate it.

Once the chartist has decided, to his satisfaction, that he has a reasonably valid trendline based upon the criteria above, he can use it for trading purposes. The trendline has, in effect, become a rising support line, as it halts each intervening minor decline. This is the reason that the line is drawn by connecting the minor bottoms and not the tops. Any penetration of that line is a cause for alarm. It would be the first sign to anyone that owns the stock that the major direction of the stock is changing. The chartist is immediately placed on his guard. The fundamental reason for the change in direction is sometimes not known for weeks or months later.

TRADING THE UPTREND

With the addition of this concept of trendline analysis, the reader is now even better equipped to trade from a technical standpoint. From the previous chapter, he learned to use broad congestion areas to improve his trading. Now, with this addition, he is able to use the chart even when the stock does not rest long enough to form such well-defined areas. Looking at figure 6-2, an uptrend can be followed from beginning to end. It may be a trend lasting two months or two years. Let us see how this stock could be traded, using no other considerations than support, resistance and trendline analysis.

Assuming that the chartist is watching this stock from the beginning, the first commitment might have been made at

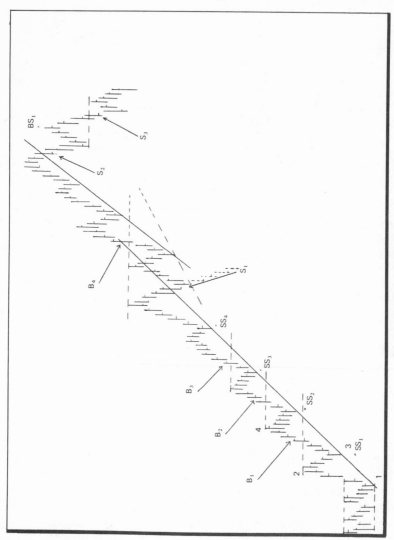

FIG. 6.2. TRADING THE UPTREND LINE.

point B_1. It is there that the minimum requirements of the trendline are met. Point 3 met the requirement of two succeeding higher minor bottoms and at B_1 the chartist is assured of having a second minor high, higher than the first at point 2 since that peak has been penetrated. A protective stop-loss order can very conveniently be placed below the previous minor bottom at SS_1, which would be the closest significant support price.

More conservative traders may wait for further tests of the trendline before taking a position. For example, at point B_2 the trendline has been tested once again, and a new high has been made by penetrating the resistance of the minor top at point 4. A new position taken at B_2 can be doubly sure of success. Once again, the position can be protected with a stop order below the last minor bottom at SS_2. The venturesome chartist who took his position at B_1 can now move his protective stop order up to SS_2. In fact, the trendline analysis here is an excellent example of how the follow-up stop order may be used most effectively. Positions may be held and protective stops moved up successively under each minor bottom as long as the uptrend remains intact. In this manner the position can be held as long as possible. The end to the uptrend must eventually come, however, and it is the chart that will give the first indication, not fundamental news. The chartist is therefore on constant alert.

The first sign of a trend reversal, with the well-established trendline as shown in figure 6-2, would be a close below the trendline. The conservative chartist would liquidate his position at that point (S_1). He might also wait, to be sure, until his stop order at at SS_4 is activated. He might also, if he is more aggressive, liquidate his long position at S_1 and, when his judgement is confirmed by a penetration of the minor bottom at SS_4, initiate a short position.

One note of caution is necessary at this point. It is true that the broken trendline signaled a change in the trend. Often, however, the change is one from an uptrend to a sideways trend or a broad congestion area. It is nevertheless a change in trend and, when the sideways movement is completed, the trend may again change to either a new downtrend or the resumption of the previous uptrend. A more venturesome trader, or one with large profits, might maintain his position until the congestion area is completed and the new trend begun. However, it is not bad charting technique to liquidate at the first penetration of the trendline, for the position can always be reinstated at B_4, the completion of the resting phase. There is always a good chance that the penetration of the trendline might be followed by a sharp decline, as the dotted line indicates, without a congestion area being formed at all. This is particularly true for the rapidly moving stock.

Very often, although the advance continues even after the trendline has been broken, as in figure 6-2, the penetration still remains as a danger signal that the trend is weakening. A general rule to follow may be that the stronger and more valid the trendline, the more meaningful is its destruction and, hence, the more caution needed. In our example, very shortly after the first congestion area, the chartist is given another chance to decide whether to follow the penetrated trendline at S_2. In this instance, the trendline penetration was not followed by a congestion area, but signaled the end of the entire advance.

Although not all stocks advance in such an orderly fashion, the number that do is surprising. When the chartist finds such a stock, the analysis above is all that is needed to follow the advance from beginning to end. It is possible that he may be forced to liquidate his position prematurely, as in this example, in which the chartist may have acted conservatively. The reader will find that the experienced chartist is always willing to give up a few points to be sure. Just how much of his profits he is willing to give up to be sure that a new downtrend is beginning is a question of the amount of risk he is willing to take. Regardless of this, the penetration of a valid trendline is a sure signal that the trend is changing. It may change to a sideways trend, as a rest or as a pause before the reversal of the trend, or it may reverse immediately upon the penetration of the trendline.

THE DOWNTREND

With a very few changes, all of the analysis above may be applied to a stock that is declining, since stocks may also

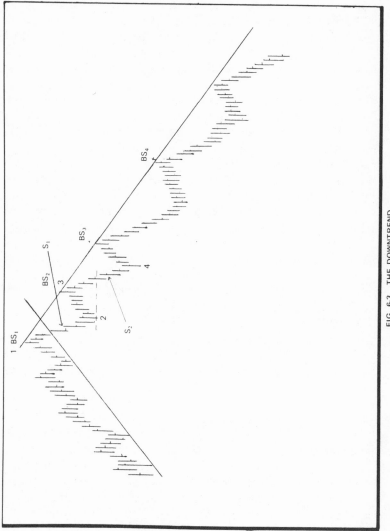

FIG. 6-3. THE DOWNTREND.

decline in an orderly manner, forming neat downward trend-lines. The downtrend, like the uptrend, is a succession of minor tops and bottoms. Each one is *lower* than the previous ones in the downtrend, however. The trendline is, in this case, a straight line connecting the minor *tops* of the move. Just as the uptrend line formed a support line above which each decline finds buying, the downtrend line forms a line of resistance at which all succeeding rallies fail.

Two minor tops and two minor bottoms are also considered the minimum requirements to draw a downtrend line. Looking at figure 6-3, the penetration of the minor bottom at S_2 signals the beginning of the downtrend, since we have a minimum number of tops and bottoms assured. The first sale may then be made at this point. If the trader had taken a short position when the previous uptrend was broken at S_1, his protective stop order could be placed just above the high point of the move at BS_1. Once the minor bottom at S_2 was penetrated, this stop order could be moved to BS_2. Any new short positions taken at S_2 should also be protected with a buy stop at BS_2. In a manner similar to that described in the discussion of the uptrend, the entire decline may be followed down with the use of a trailing protective stop, placed above each succeeding minor top until the decline is finally ended.

The short sales can be covered or new purchases made at the first signs of a reversal of the downtrend. This will also begin with a penetration of the trendline, this time by a rally. The same risks of the stock first moving into a congestion area are possible in this situation also. However, one important signal is present in the completion of the downtrend that is not present when the uptrend is ending. There is an old saying that stocks need volume to rise but may fall from their own weight. This is always the case in charting. If there is comparatively high volume on the day that the upside penetration of the trendline is made, it is much more likely to be valid reversal of the trend. An upside penetration of the trendline accompanied by very light volume should caution the trader to wait for more evidence before acting. This is not the case when the uptrend line is being broken. The breakdown may be equally valid with or without increased volume on penetration.

As the reader has seen, with the aid of charts the trader should be able to trade stocks with equal facility from the long side or from the short side. If he is patient, he will find stocks that move in an orderly fashion, like those in the two examples. The well-ordered uptrend line is very common. When stocks are declining, however, they usually fall quite rapidly, so that the well-ordered decline is rarer. When a well-ordered downtrend *is* found, it is usually a very reliable pattern.

PSYCHOLOGY OF TRENDLINE TRADING

Anyone who has traded in securities will agree that it is much easier to purchase a stock than to decide the best time to sell it. Very few traders are able to hold their positions long enough to profit by the major portion of any move. Most often, they are frightened out with a small profit during one of the minor reactions that must occur periodically within the trend. These small profits would be adequate, except for the fact that the losses, when they occur, are usually much larger than the average profit and tend to more than cancel out all of the gains. As a result, the often-heard advice of "cut your losses short and let your profits run" has become trite. Most traders agree on the soundness of the advice, but would like to know how to accomplish it.

It is much easier to become objective about a position if a picture is available. When the trader can see that these minor fluctuations are simply a part of a larger pattern his job is half done. Not only does he become more objective, he also has, as the reader has seen, a logical place for all stop orders. With this combination, he is well on his way to improving his results. Once the principles of support and resistance and trendline analysis are mastered, more refinements can be made to chart trading.

Chapter 7
REVERSAL PATTERNS

Before proceeding to further refinement, let us summarize the charting theory discussed up to this point. It has been seen that there is much more order in the price fluctuations of stocks than is apparent at a casual glance. Using charts, the trader can see through minor fluctuations to the major underlying moves which can often be identified by straight line trends in either direction. The moves may also be punctuated by sizable sideways congestion areas. The aim of any chartist should be to profit from as much of these major movements as possible. This requires that he take his position as early as possible and maintain it through minor fluctuations until the major move has finally been reversed. The charts are invaluable in this respect, as they help him to see each of the minor reactions from the major trend in their proper perspective as a necessary part of the move. It is on these minor reactions that most traders are frightened out prematurely. The charts will also aid the chartist in discerning the first signs of decay in the movement.

The broken trendline is one of these early signs. The direct changeover from one trend to the opposite, however, is not the most common type of trend reversal. Most often, after the trendline is broken a broad congestion area is formed. This is similar to many others formed during the move that turned out to be merely resting phases within the major move. This final congestion area, unlike its predecessors, turns out to be a reversal of the trend. At the end of the uptrend, it is the congestion area in which a sufficient number of buyers cannot be mustered to stem the selling of the profit-takers. In the case of the dying downtrend, everyone who is going to sell has sold, and the buyers finally take control.

Is there any way to be forewarned of this reversal? How can this congestion pattern be distinguished from the others? These questions will be answered in the pages that follow if we look more closely at the shapes of the congestion areas. Chartists have, over the years, classified many of these patterns into certain shapes that tend to repeat themselves. Not only do these similar patterns tend to form repeatedly but the price behavior that follows the completion of the patterns tends also to be uniform. That is, the price behavior of the stock can be predicted from the shape of some common patterns. The first group of patterns, described in this chapter, are the patterns that are most likely to form just at the end of a long trend. Since what follows the completion of these patterns is a trend in a new direction, they are appropriately called "reversal patterns." We will discuss each of them in turn.

DOUBLE TOPS

The first of such reversal patterns is called the "double top." It is found at the end of a long major uptrend. When a valid double top is formed, its completion signals the beginning of a major decline.

DESCRIPTION

The first of the two tops is seen as a high-volume rally, climaxing the long upward move. As the stock is driving to a new all-time high price, the volume of trading is frequently the highest total recorded for the entire move. Following the new high, a substantial decline clearly leaves a sharp peak. Since this decline usually finds support at a previous trend-line or support area, the trader still has no clue as to a pending reversal. Since major tops are often made with extremely high volume, the volume on this first peak might be the first clue, but it is not enough.

The volume that accompanies the rally to the second top is also high, but less than that of the first top. The first major sell signal is given as this rally reaches a climax short of making a new high. The sell-off then begins. In terms of support and resistance, the resistance of the first top area was greater than the buying force of the second rally. If the stock has had a well-formed uptrend line, the second major sell signal is given shortly after the failure to make a new high, as the trendline is broken. Many traders may liquidate any long

61

positions at this signal while awaiting a further indication before selling short. At this point there should be suspicion that a double top is forming, although it is not yet complete. The final sell signal, and the completion of the pattern, occurs when the support area between the two tops is penetrated on a closing basis. Once the support of this minor bottom fails to hold, the double top is complete, the uptrend has definitely been reversed and a downtrend of major proportions should be expected. Frequently, however, the stock will experience one final rally, which serves as a test of the pattern. This rally, occurring shortly after the completion of the pattern, will fall just short of penetrating the minor bottom of the formation. Once again, the theory of support and resistance is seen at work. The support of the minor bottom, having been penetrated, serves as resistance to this minor rally. Since the stock is too weak to penetrate this significant area, there is a final confirmation of the reversal. This final testing rally, which is found in most patterns, is called a "pullback." The volume should be light on this pullback.

TRADING THE DOUBLE TOP

There are a number of different ways to take advantage of the double top. Looking at figure 7-1, the reader will see several selling opportunities. The first sell signal is the penetration of the uptrend line. A long position may be liquidated here if the trendline was particularly well formed. Although a dangerous trade, a short position may be taken with a close protective buy stop above the second peak at BS_1. Certainly, all long positions should be liquidated at S_2, the completion of the pattern. A short position taken there would also be protected at BS_1. Finally, most short positions should be taken with the failure of the pullback. The short position should not be taken until the pullback has definitely failed and the stock has turned down again. The stop may then be placed at BS_2, just above the final peak of the pullback. Finally, the penetration of the minor low prior to the pullback at S_4 signals the beginning of the new downtrend, which serves as a further selling opportunity.

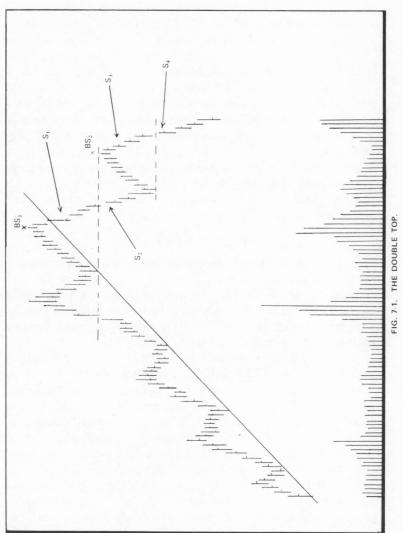

FIG. 7.1. THE DOUBLE TOP.

A NOTE OF CAUTION

A few words of caution may be necessary at this point for the beginning chartist. It seems that every beginning chartist starts out by discovering many more patterns than there actually are. Good advice for him, at the outset, is to be overcritical of each pattern. Make doubly sure that each suspected pattern meets every requirement of the ideal pattern. The more closely the pattern resembles the ideal, the more likely it is to work. For example, the double top should appear as a distinct double top. There should be two very sharp peaks with extremely high volume, especially on the first peak. The peaks should stand out, with a sell-off between the peaks of at least 10 to 15%. The peaks should both top out at nearly the same price. Finally, it should be a large pattern with the peaks at least a month or two apart. Remember, this pattern portends a decline of magnitude. Tops found only several days apart are meaningless.

DOUBLE BOTTOMS

The double bottom is, in most respects, exactly the reverse of the pattern just discussed. It is a very common reversal pattern found as the final congestion area of a long major decline. The move that follows this pattern, like the double top, is of major proportions. It is likewise a broad pattern formed over a period of months.

The first bottom is made as the stock moves down into new low ground. The volume accompanying this selling is often very high and the daily declines very sharp. It is often the worst sell-off of the entire decline. When the bottom is finally made, the rally that follows is weak and lacking volume. The lack of volume is the clue that the reversal is not yet at hand. If the stock has declined in an orderly fashion, this rally often ends, as in figure 7-2, at the trendline. Should it penetrate the trendline slightly, it would not be significant, since the rally has little volume.

The decline that now follows gives the chartist his first signals of the impending reversal. This sell-off, although also quite sharp, lacks much of the volume force of the first, and the price does not drop so precipitously. This first signal of

64

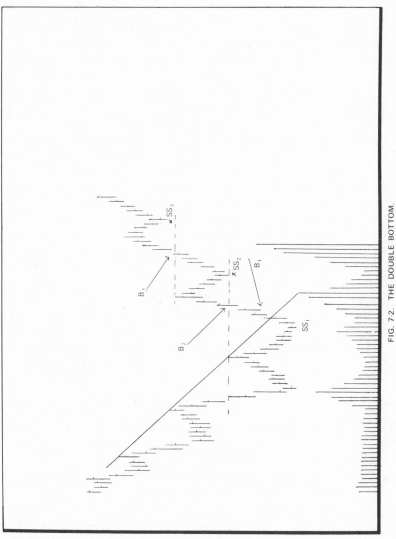

FIG. 7-2. THE DOUBLE BOTTOM.

the weakening downtrend is confirmed when the stock is not able to make a new low and, instead, begins to rally following this successful test of the support of the old low. This test, together with the lighter volume of the second decline, is a testimony to the growing strength of the stock.

The rally from the second bottom immediately gives the chartist the third buy signal. The volume accompanying this rally is much higher than that of the previous rally. For the first time, the stock appears to be trying to stage a substantial rally. The volume steadily increases as the stock moves away from the second bottom. Very shortly, the successful upside penetration of the trendline adds another buy signal. At this point, many venturesome chartists are taking their first positions or at least, are covering outstanding short sales. The more conservative chartist would await the final test before adding new long positions. All doubt is finally removed when the rally, with high volume, penetrates the resistance of the minor top between the two bottoms. With a close beyond this point, the pattern is complete.

Once more, a pullback to the pattern is a possibility as a final test to the pattern. The volume characteristics are quite important on this pullback if it is to be a confirmation of the "breakout." While the stock is pulling back to the pattern, the volume should be extremely light in comparison to that of the breakout rally. The resistance of the minor top, which served as the resistance test to the breakout, is now support for the ensuing pullback. When the pullback fails to break below this support point and, instead, turns to rally sharply with high volume, another strong buying signal is given. Frequently, the trading after the pullback is even higher than that evident while the stock was breaking out of its pattern.

TRADING THE DOUBLE BOTTOM

The trading procedure with the double bottom is very similar to that used with the double top. The first clear buy signal is given by the penetration of the trendline at B_1. At this point, the covering of any short sales is a wise precaution. Although a long commitment here might be premature, if one is taken it should be protected with a stop order below the second bottom at SS_1. More aggressive long positions can be taken at the breakout point at B_2, also with stop protection at SS_1. If the breakout is missed, additional positions may be taken after the successful pullback at B_3, which also confirms the beginning of a new uptrend. Protective stop orders may now be raised to SS_2.

DOUBLE TOPS AND BOTTOMS COMPARED

Now that the reader has been exposed to the first pair of reversal patterns, it would be helpful to pause to compare them. Most of the comparisons will apply to all reversal patterns, since most top reversal patterns have their mirror image bottom patterns. There are, however, a few differences.

The most important difference lies in the volume characteristics, reflecting the saying that stocks need volume to rise. At the breakout from the double top pattern high volume is not a prerequisite, while the breakout from the double bottom should be suspected if not accompanied by extremely high volume. The differences concerning the volume accompanying the pullbacks in each case have already been mentioned.

A note of caution is also needed on pullbacks. While pullbacks are a useful confirmation of the breakout, they are not always present following the completion of patterns. They often do not occur when the stock is breaking out *with* the market. That is, an upside breakout that occurs within the atmosphere of an extremely strong overall market will very likely carry a considerable distance from the breakout point before finally sustaining any correction. The same point may apply to a downside breakout that occurs during a sharp market decline. Consequently, as a matter of trading procedure, a trader should not put himself into a position in which he can sustain a loss while awaiting a pullback. For example, with the completion of a double top, he should liquidate any longs at the breakout and should not wait for a pullback. He may wait for the pullback to initiate a new short position, when its failure to occur would cost him only a missed trade.

There are several differences in shape between top and bottom patterns. The double top, for example, will tend to have very sharp peaks, while the double bottom will tend to cover a greater distance and also may be more rounded. This

67

general difference exists between most top and bottom patterns.

The reversal patterns of this chapter are all harbingers of major moves and not merely of short-term rallies or declines. It may also be noted that with the double top and bottom, as well as with most patterns, the chartist never catches the bottom or top. He must always be willing to give up a few points to be sure of the trend change. It is in this way that charts help to keep the trader in a position to profit from as much of the major moves as possible. Although the trader may try to cut down these points by taking positions before the actual breakout and completion of the pattern, he is always taking more risk. Since these patterns usually portend major moves, the few extra points given are only good insurance.

HEAD AND SHOULDERS—TOP

Probably the most powerful and best known of all reversal patterns is the "head and shoulders" formation. It has frequently been the culprit in many long, disastrous declines. When it is found in the popular stock averages, the beginning of a new bear market decline is imminent. This formation, very common in the latter stages of a major market advance, is indeed the harbinger of major declines. When a number of them are found in a collection of charts, there is concern for the market as a whole.

DESCRIPTION

During the formation of the head and shoulders pattern, several important sell signals are given which are, in themselves, sufficient warning of an impending decline. When the chartist has found a valid pattern that conforms to all of the conditions described below, he has a very reliable trading tool that he should not fail to heed.

The first rally of the pattern is formed as the stock pushes to a new high, accompanied by extremely high volume. Like all major top reversal patterns, it is preceded by a major advance in prices. The sell-off that follows is one of normal profit-taking that violates no significant support area and will usually hold at the trendline if one can be distinguished.

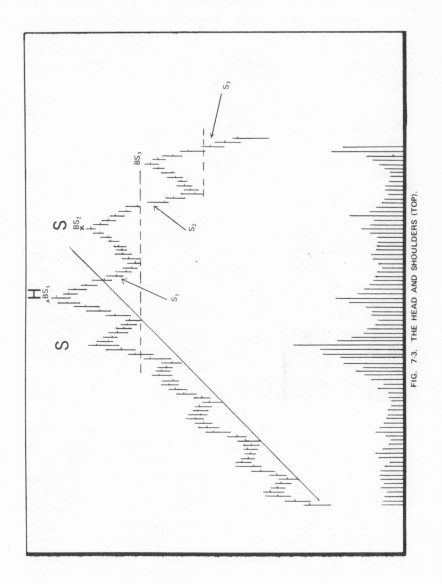

FIG. 7·3. THE HEAD AND SHOULDERS (TOP).

Although, as yet, the chartist has no reason to suspect it, the left shoulder of the pattern has been formed.

The second rally of the pattern, unlike the double top, manages to set a new high price for the stock. The volume on this rally, however, is much lighter than that on the first and the rally does not seem quite as forceful as the first. This is the first sign of weakness in the trend. The "head" of the pattern has now been formed.

The decline from this new high gives the next significant signs of the decaying advance. The selling is much more spirited and the stock fails to stop at the trendline. It is here that the trader might first begin to suspect the head and shoulders formation and, at least, a reversal of some type. The penetration of the trendline may be the first occasion for liquidation. If a true head and shoulders is forming, this decline will end at the same price area as the decline from the left shoulder, leaving a twice-tested support area. The next rally from this point will help to decide the issue.

As the stock begins its third rally of the pattern, the alert chartist should be watching carefully for a confirmation of his suspicions. This rally contains a number of important signals. First, the rally is generally very weak, with light volume and sluggish price movement. It not only fails to make a new high, which is in itself a bearish signal, but it does not even have the strength to penetrate the resistance of the left shoulder. With this additional sell signal the trader should be growing certain of the pattern. This rally is often the pullback to the broken uptrend line. As the stock then begins to decline once more, it leaves behind the "right shoulder." For the conservative chartist, there is one remaining test—the support area of the two previous declines. A line connecting the bottoms of these two rallies is called the "neckline." Once the stock closes below this neckline, the pattern is completed and the last of the long positions should be liquidated. Although the stock has already fallen a number of points from the top of the head, there is still enough selling ahead to warrant liquidation.

For those who missed the breakout or who wish to initiate new short positions, there is one more opportunity and test. It is, of course, the pullback which should occur with very light volume. The resistance area of the now-penetrated neckline should prove to be too strong for this rally and the major decline should then begin.

Because this pattern is also a major trend reversal formation, it must not be expected to form over a period of several days or even weeks. It is a pattern that will build over a period of months and is often better distinguished on weekly charts.

TRADING THE PATTERN

By now, the reader is becoming familiar with the techniques of trading with reversal patterns. The first selling might be done as the trendline is broken at S_1. This is especially useful for the trader who has the multiple position. He might begin to lighten up here but wait for further confirmation before proceeding. The riskier short sale made at this point should most assuredly be protected with a stop order at BS_1, slightly above the head of the pattern. Selling must be done at S_2, since the pattern is then complete and a new downtrend has been confirmed. Short sales made may be protected with buy stop orders above the right shoulder at BS_2. Finally, sales may again be made at S_3, after the failure of the pullback and upon the further confirmation of the new downtrend.

HEAD AND SHOULDERS—BOTTOM

The bottom counterpart of this formation is usually powerful and reliable. It is, however, often more difficult to distinguish than the top formation. Because overall volume and interest in the market is usually much lower at the end of a bear market, the activity during the formation of the bottom pattern tends to be much less than at the top. Because of this, the pattern tends to be smaller and flatter. Other characteristics are similar.

The left shoulder of this pattern is usually made on relatively high volume, while the rally that follows the low is a feeble one. It ends at the trendline. The stock then descends into new low territory, but this time with much lighter trading. The rally that follows the formation of the head is much more spirited than the previous one but still lacks conviction.

71

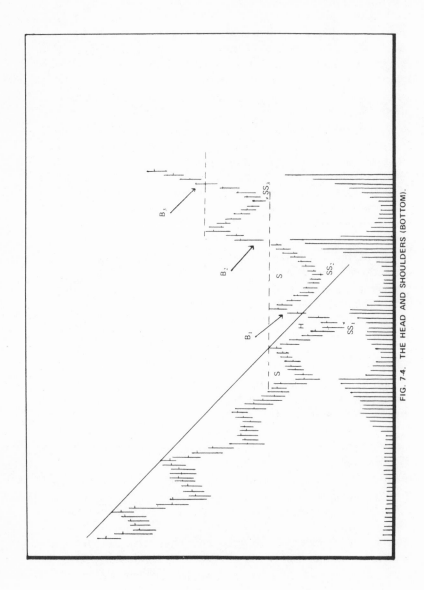

FIG. 7.4. THE HEAD AND SHOULDERS (BOTTOM).

Because this rally penetrates the downtrend line, the chartist should take notice. The first of any short sales outstanding might be covered here at B_1. The rally falters, however, at the same point of resistance as the first rally from the left shoulder. The next decline gives the first clear buy signal of the pattern. It finds support in the area of the left shoulder and, with light volume, does not even test the lows of the move before it suddenly turns up again. This is usually the cue for an explosion in the volume. The stock moves quickly in heavy trading to the breakout point, which is the area of resistance of the two previous rallies or the neckline of the pattern. A close beyond the neckline, with high volume, completes the right shoulder and the pattern. It also confirms the beginning of a new uptrend. Any short sales that were not covered at the penetration of the trendline must now be covered. New long positions taken here at B_2 can be protected with a sell stop order at SS_2, just below the bottom of the right shoulder. Any previous stops at SS_1 may now also be moved up.

Traders may then watch the pattern for the pullback as a test of the breakout and an opportunity to add to their positions. The pullback should once again occur with very light trading, finding support at the penetrated neckline which is now a support area. The rally that follows the successful test of the neckline support should feature another burst of high volume and rapidly advancing prices. The new positions may be taken as the stock surpasses its previous minor top preceding the pullback at B_3, while all stop orders may now be moved up to SS_3.

Because the head and shoulders patterns are usually popular with beginning chartists, it is again necessary to caution the reader on several points. This pattern is a broad and significant pattern that, like the double tops and bottoms, forms over a period of months. They are both usually found either at the end of a bull market or a bear market. Finally, the most reliable patterns are those that satisfy not only the requirements of shape but also volume.

THE BASE PATTERN

An easy reversal pattern to understand is the "base," for the stock that is making a base acts in a very logical manner.

It is one instance in which the stock acts just as the fundamentals do. For example, a company that has falling earnings for one fundamental reason or another must eventually decline. After a long decline in earnings, the company must eventually reach a point where its problems can get no worse or it will go out of business. Assuming the company will turn around, sooner or later its cost-cutting program, management shakeup or other drastic measures must bear fruit. During the problem period, the price of its stock is naturally falling until it too reaches a bottom. The price will then move sideways in a narrow trading range with very small volume as traders lose interest. It has now become a waiting game. The stock has formed a dormant base pattern. The stock will break out of its base when the fundamentals of the company finally improve. In fact, as we know, the stock will begin to move in price long before the news of the fundamental improvement is made public. This is the popular "turn around" situation that is the favorite advertisement of stock advisory services. The very logic of the price action appeals to traders, as well as the seemingly limited risk because the stock is so thoroughly "sold out." In spite of this popularity, logic and limited risk, there is probably more money lost on this pattern than all the others we have mentioned to this point.

The most common mistake made by chartists is that they try to guess at the turnaround instead of letting the chart reveal it. The mere existence of the base pattern is not a reason for short-term traders to take a long position. It is the *completion* of the pattern that should concern them. Instead, many traders will take their positions as soon as they discover a base, hoping that a breakout will soon occur. They reason that the risk is small since the stock has obviously bottomed out, and they need only wait. Frequently, however, the base may last for a year or longer. Eventually, in these cases, the trader sells from boredom and, although his losses may be small, his valuable trading funds were tied up. There is also the additional risk that the base does not mark the low but merely a resting phase before a further decline. Since the company is obviously not a dynamic situation at that time, this is not an unreasonable expectation. This is always a distinct possibility until the stock finally completes the pattern by an upside breakout.

74

The chartist is not alone among the victims of this type of pattern. It is a very common mistake among fundamental traders to make purchases simply because the stock has fallen sharply and seems to be finally at a bottom.

TRADING THE PATTERN

It is not difficult to trade the base pattern correctly. The chart in figure 7-5 is very typical example of the dormant base. Because this pattern is popular there are, at times, false moves during the formation of the base. These are the sharp moves out of the base with a sudden flareup in volume. Usually, the stock falls back into the base very quickly. These breakouts are probably the only risks of misinterpreting the pattern. The true breakout from the dormant base pattern that signals the beginning of an extended upward move is usually easy to differentiate from the false starts. The true breakout closes well beyond the highest point of the entire base trading range, with the highest volume of the entire basing period. Even more important than this volume, however, is the trading that precedes the breakout. There is, invariably, a very evident volume buildup that starts weeks before the breakout actually occurs. This is in direct contrast to the false breakout that characteristically materializes very quickly and disappears just as fast. If the company is experiencing a turnaround in its corporate fortunes, certainly many people close to the firm will know of the good news and begin to buy the stock. As the news and rumors grow, the volume gradually mounts. Finally, as the news release is imminent, the volume is beginning to reach its height and the stock is just breaking out. Once again, the alert chartist is in his position well before the news is released. The true breakout will anticipate the actual fundamental news and not appear without reason, as is the case in most false breakouts.

The trading strategy is simple. The first long positions should be taken only when the stock closes well beyond the upper limits of the base with proper volume. A stop order may be placed below the base at SS_1. The next positions may be taken after the breakout has been tested by a valid pullback, with light volume, and then confirmed by a new high for the move at B_2. Stop orders may now be moved up to SS_2.

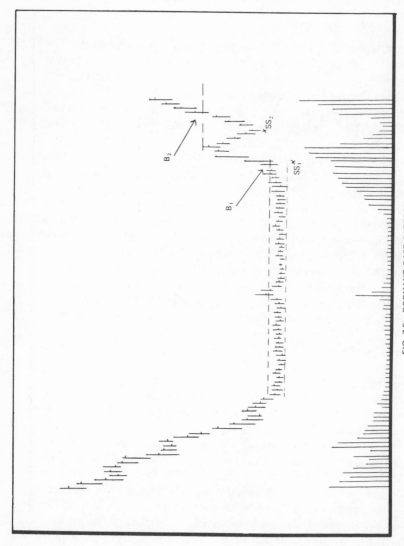

FIG. 7·5. DORMANT BASE PATTERN.

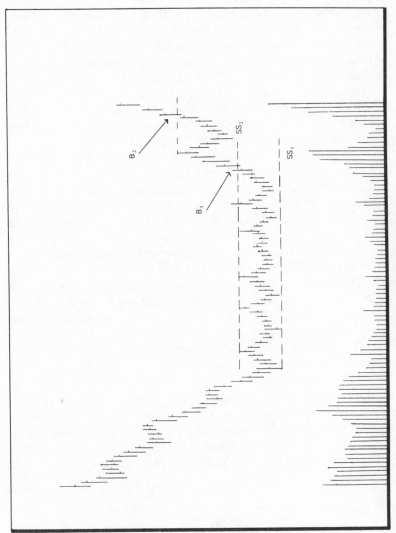

FIG. 7-6. BASE VARIATION.

A VARIATION

The base described above is usually found in stocks in which fundamental problems are serious and lack of interest prolonged. There are a number of variations of this base principle that are equally helpful to the trader as an indicator of trend reversals. Figure 7-6 depicts a situation very similar to the previous base. The performance of the stock during this base is not nearly as lifeless but it is still a base formation. With this type of base, the troubles of the firm are neither so prolonged nor as serious as that experienced by the first firm. This base is shorter and the volume, on average, much higher. The stock has not been depressed long enough for the trading interest to wane as much as in the dormant base.

Although the stock does not stay in the tight range as before, there is usually some resistance point evident at the top of the price range, as well as definable support at some point at the bottom of the range. Very often, these points are so clear-cut that straight lines may be drawn connecting the minor tops of all rallies and the minor bottoms of each sell-off. Thus there is a well-defined trading range from which a breakout will eventually occur. The helpful clue of the volume buildup is not quite so evident in this pattern because of the more frequent rallies with their higher volume. Nevertheless, the true breakout will be evident as the resistance line is broken accompanied by high volume. The tendency for a technical pullback is also present in this variation and the trading strategy is the same.

This second type of base is probably more common than the dormant variety and much more likely to forecast a much smaller, short-term move. There is also the greater possibility that it will act more as a resting phase within the trend rather than a reversal of the trend. In fact, the very short base of this type resembles the rectangle pattern to be discussed in the next chapter.

LINE TOP

Many charting texts describe a line top which resembles the dormant base mentioned above, except that it appears at the end of a long upward movement. It would be the bull market counterpart to the base described. The formation is so rare, however, that it is best to ignore it. There is also very little logic behind the pattern in terms of fundamental actions. Traders will not sit patiently, waiting for the fortunes of the company to worsen, as a stock moves sideways with light trading. Once the upward momentum of the company is stalled, the stock generally begins to fall, perhaps forming a quick reversal pattern of another type. A short base of the second type mentioned may be formed after an uptrend, but it will be described in the coming chapter as a rectangle. When a line top is found, it is likely to be in the very high-priced and slow moving types of stocks that most traders do not follow because they are poor trading vehicles.

OTHER REVERSAL PATTERNS

There are several other reversal patterns mentioned in many charting texts that might be mentioned briefly here. They are patterns that, in the opinion of the author, are either too rare or better classified as other patterns. These appear in figure 7-7.

SAUCER BOTTOM

The saucer or rounding bottom is a reversal pattern quite similar to the dormant base. Those fundamental conditions that resulted in the formation of the base pattern discussed above are also present in the firm that forms the saucer bottom. The pattern, although very rare, is usually found in low-priced stocks. The volume characteristics, like the shape of the pattern, also form a saucer shape, with the dullest trading in the middle of the pattern.

A line drawn across the top of the pattern as if it were a top for the saucer is the critical point for a breakout. Once this line is breached, with high volume, the pattern is complete, and long positions may be taken with a protective stop order below the bottom of the saucer. Although the trading tactics are similar to that of the base, it is easy to see that it is much more difficult to exactly distinguish the true breakout point.

ROUNDING TOP

The rounding top, as a top counterpart to the saucer bottom, is even rarer, if possible. If one is found, it is very

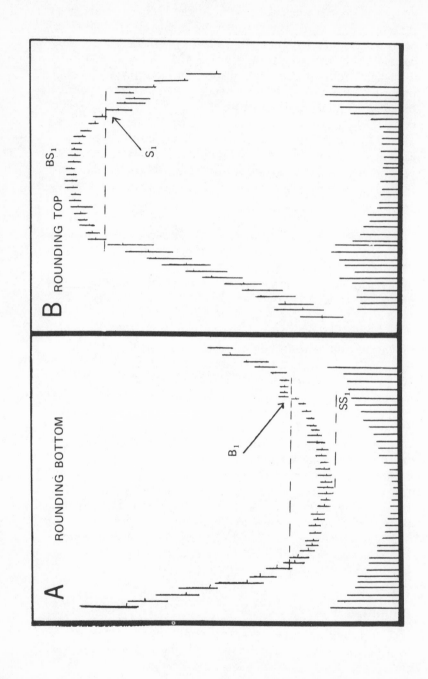

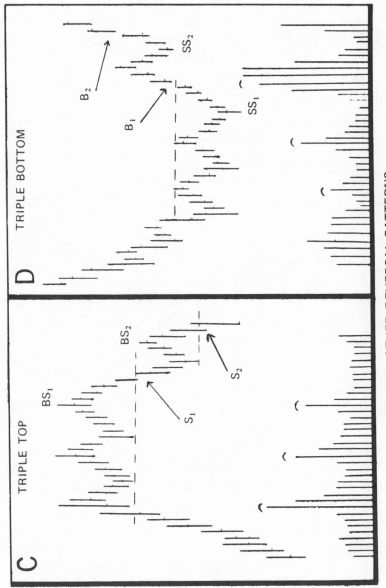

FIG. 7-7. OTHER REVERSAL PATTERNS.

likely to be formed, once again, in the high-priced, quiet-trading stock. The trading implications are exactly the opposite to those of the saucer bottom, except for the now familiar volume prerequisite for the upside breakout. It is mentioned here only to complete the list of often-mentioned but seldom-seen reversal patterns.

MULTIPLE TOPS AND BOTTOMS

Many charting texts also make separate mention of the "triple top" and the "triple bottom," although they deserve little extra attention, in that they may be considered as extensions or variations of the double top or double bottom. They may also be analyzed as the rectangle pattern to be considered in the following chapter.

If analyzed as an extension of the double top or bottom pattern, the same theory and trading procedure applies. In the top formation, each of the three tops would find its high at roughly the same price and the volume would be less on each rally, testifying to the growing weakness of the stock. Instead of having only one intervening minor bottom to test for support, the breakout point will be a twice-tested support price. The pattern would be complete only when this support area is broken. In the triple bottom, as in the double bottom, each decline will diminish in strength, and each intervening rally will gather more lively trading and movement until the breakout will finally occur when the high point of the two previous rallies is surpassed. In other words, it is the same as the double patterns, with only an additional minor top or minor bottom being added.

It is also possible to see four or more minor tops or minor bottoms in the patterns, in which case the analysis above need only be extended again. It is much easier, however, to consider the patterns as rectangles, as we will shortly see.

SUMMARY OF REVERSAL PATTERNS

The reader now has the major ingredients of a charting system. He is acquainted with the basic notion of support and resistance as the foundation of most charting theory. He knows that stock trends can be long and orderly. He also knows that the orderly progression of the stock can be interrupted often by congestion areas, as normal profit-taking occurs. One of these patterns, however, will prove to be the undoing of the stock and will reverse the entire trend. This is the reversal pattern, an important timing tool. Most of these patterns are shapeless and quite similar to many preceding congestion areas. It will only be apparent to the chartist that the trend is being reversed when an important support or resistance area within the pattern is penetrated. The size of these patterns is often the best key to the magnitude of the decline or advance to follow. Quite naturally, the larger the pattern usually the more significant is the reversal to follow.

The task of distinguishing the reversal from the congestion pattern that is merely a pause in the trend has been greatly simplified over the years. Chartists have gradually compiled a list of important reversal patterns that consistently take familiar shapes. The most common and reliable of these patterns have been discussed in this chapter. When the chartist discovers a congestion pattern that conforms to the requirements listed for each pattern, he can be confident of the reversal to follow. Each of the patterns discussed are harbingers of new major trends. Because they are necessarily broad patterns that form over many months, they are often more readily apparent on weekly charts. As an aid to identifying these major reversal patterns, it must be remembered that there must always exist a major move for these patterns to reverse. Too often, beginning chartists claim the discovery of a head and shoulders, for example, on a chart that shows nothing but a long sideways movement of the stock. All of these patterns are found only at the end of a long major advance or decline.

Finally, let us consider the reversal that gives very little advance warning and forms no major congestion pattern first. Very often, the only signal is the penetration of a trendline. These are, of course, very difficult to analyze. This problem exists usually in stocks that have very rapid moves and which then reverse themselves in the same manner. A separate chapter has been set aside to discuss this problem.

In the next chapter, the final addition to a system of charting will be discussed. It will deal with those congestion patterns found within the trend that do not turn out to be reversal patterns. They are merely resting or "consolidation" phases within the major trend. A number of recurring shapes have also been categorized among these patterns, a knowledge of which will give the trader a much greater insight into continuation congestion areas.

Chapter 8
CONSOLIDATION PATTERNS

Now that the reader is prepared for the beginning and the end of the market trend, it only remains that he become proficient with all that passes between. Within this middle-ground there may be any number of sudden interruptions of the trend, each one bringing a fresh challenge to the trader. It is here that most trading mistakes are made, for it is during these unexpected pauses that traders with small profits scurry for cover, only to miss the major move still to follow.

It has been seen already that these congestion areas, or resting phases which the chartist calls "consolidations," are beneficial. It is exactly this process of removing stock from the weak hands of the nervous trader that breathes new life into the trend. For this reason, the stock that has consolidated and then breaks out to continue its trend does so with renewed vigor. Without these pauses, the trend becomes increasingly vulnerable to the fatal reversal. Once again, charts can be used to see these consolidations objectively rather than with trepidation. Without the benefit of the over-all picture afforded by a chart, the average trader becomes nervous whenever his stock hesitates in its forward progress.

The reader has seen how a closer examination of the reversing congestion patterns revealed a number of helpful recurring formations. A closer study of the consolidating congestion patterns will also uncover a number of recurring shapes that soon become familiar friends. A knowledge of these formations will be just as helpful as the reversal patterns of the previous chapter. They will enable the trader to avoid premature profit-taking and, if he missed the beginning of the move, will help him select logical places to take positions within the trend. In this chapter and the next, the most common of these consolidation patterns will be explored.

TRIANGLES

The triangle is the most prevalent of all the consolidation patterns. Like most of the consolidation patterns to be discussed, the triangle is usually a pause within the continuing trend. On occasion, however, it will prove to be a reversing pattern. Naturally, an important part of their analysis will be to distinguish between the two.

Because triangles are merely continuation patterns as a rule, they are usually smaller than the average reversal formation and will form in much less time, and also appear much more frequently. Since the patterns are smaller, the moves that they forecast are minor in nature. The triangles simply forecast the minor price swings within the primary trend. Although there are large variations between each individual triangle, most of the patterns will fall into one of three shapes: the ascending right triangle, the descending right triangle, and the symmetrical triangle. The first has bullish implications, the second bearish, and the third is indifferent. Each will be discussed separately, although we will see that all are similar.

SYMMETRICAL TRIANGLE

DESCRIPTION

The symmetrical triangle is formed by a succession of minor rallies and declines. There is a regularity to the rallies, in that a line drawn connecting each of the tops will result in a short-term downtrend line. The bottoms of each decline, when similarly connected, will form a short-term uptrend line. The two lines converge to form a perfectly symmetrical triangle. Since two points are always needed to draw a straight line, the chartist requires, as a minimum, two minor tops and two minor bottoms in order to construct a triangle, although there may be several more points testing the lines so drawn.

The symmetrical triangle represents a pitched battle between the forces of supply and demand in which both sides seem to be evenly matched. Each rally is unable to carry through to a new high and tops out below the high of the previous rally. But the sellers are no stronger, as each decline finds a bottom at a slightly higher level. It is impossible to forecast, in advance, which side will succeed. Only the completion of the pattern will tell the story; and it is completed

86

when the stock finally closes beyond the confines of the chart, which are the minor converging trendlines. The larger the pattern and the greater number of times each of the trendlines is tested, the more valid will be the implications of the triangle. Once the valid triangle is completed, a substantial movement in the direction of the breakout will occur.

VOLUME

The first of the four points required for the construction of the triangle formed within an uptrend is the highest price for the stock within the entire triangle. (See the first triangle in figure 8-1.) Since this top represents the strongest rally of the congestion area, it should also have the highest volume of trading. The ideal triangle formation will always begin this way. The highest volume should occur at the beginning of the pattern and should then gradually diminish as the pattern progresses toward completion. This is a logical development, since each succeeding rally and decline is less powerful than the preceding one. The volume characteristics are similar for the symmetrical triangle found within the downtrend. The first construction point, however, will always be the lowest point reached during the pattern, which will also be on the first in volume.

The breakout from the pattern should occur well before the apex of the triangle is reached, usually somewhere beyond the halfway point within the triangle. The volume accompanying this breakout once again conforms to the general rule previously given. That is, the upside breakout must be accompanied by a substantial increase in trading that very abruptly ends the gradually declining trend of volume within the pattern. Although the downside breakout does not necessarily require this substantial change to establish its validity, it usually does carry with it a much larger trading volume than any of the days immediately preceding it.

The final volume characteristic of the symmetrical triangle, that accompanying the possible pullback, conforms to the same rules as those applying to pullbacks with the previous formations discussed. Following the upside breakout with its high volume, the pullback should offer a marked decrease in trading in comparison. It is then followed by a sudden in-

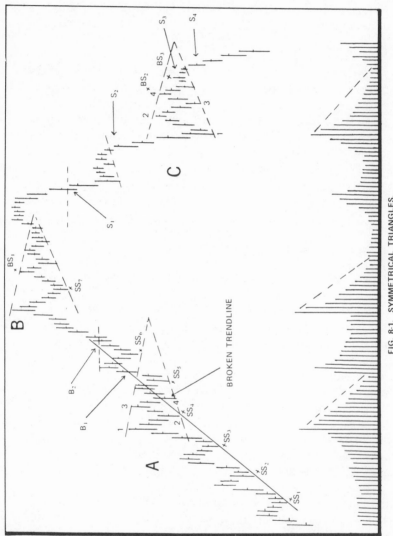

FIG. 8-1. SYMMETRICAL TRIANGLES.

crease in volume as the pullback is completed and another rally follows. With the downside breakout, although high downside volume is not needed on the breakout, the pullback should especially demonstrate very dull trading while the decline that follows the rallying pullback usually attracts more selling than the original breakout.

TRADING

The trading possibilities of the symmetrical triangle, as well as other consolidation formation, differ from the tactics used with the reversal patterns. The consolidation pattern is usually an aid to the continuation of the trend rather than spelling the destruction of it. Unlike the reversal pattern, it should not frighten the trader out of his position prematurely but, rather, should encourage him to hold until the completion of the pattern, for the rally or decline that follows the successful completion of the formation is usually large enough to reward the patient holder handsomely for his wait. If it were not for the fact that these formations sometimes turn out to be reversal patterns, the chartist would do well to take a position as soon as the formation of a consolidation pattern is suspected. By waiting for the breakout he would only be losing potential profits. Until later in this book, when hints are given on how to anticipate a breakout, the prudent course is always to await the final outcome of the pattern. Looking at figure 8-1, the reader may see the three situations in which he might find a symmetrical triangle.

In triangle A, the formation appears as an interruption of an uptrend. The trader who already has a long position has several alternatives. If he has been following the uptrend with stop orders under each minor bottom, he might continue the procedure and avoid being stopped out until the pattern finally breaks out on the downside. He might also, conservatively, sell out his position when the trendline is broken, as in the example, on the minor decline leading to the second bottom of the triangle. He might then reinstate his position only if the pattern is completed by an upside breakout. Usually, however, the trader should already have a strong suspicion of the triangle formation at this point. Finally, the trader may simply hold his position until the pattern is complete and add to his long position on the breakout. All long positions can then be protected with a stop order below the last minor bottom of the triangle at SS_5.

For the trader who has a short position when the triangle is being formed, the tactics are different. Because the odds are in favor of a continuation of the rising trend, he cannot afford to take as many chances as the long trader. The first course for him is to await the breakout and completion of the suspected triangle and if on the upside, liquidate his short position immediately. To cut his losses somewhat, he might carry a protective buy stop order just above the point at which the upside breakout might occur to liquidate just as soon as the upper trendline of the pattern is penetrated. A second prudent course to follow, especially if the pattern is a particularly good one, would be a liquidation of the position before the completion of the pattern, since the odds favor an upside breakout. The position can be easily reinstated if the triangle turns out to be a reversal pattern. A sell stop might even be placed under the lower trendline of the triangle to make sure that the position is reinstated at the downside breakout.

The trader who has no position at all represents the final trading possibility for this triangle. Because the symmetrical triangle, unlike the right triangle to be discussed, gives no advance indication of the direction of the breakout, the most prudent course for this trader is to do nothing until completion of the formation. Of all the triangles, the symmetrical triangle is the most likely to reverse the trend and fool the impatient trader who moves in too early.

Triangle B depicts a different story altogether. It is the more unusual situation, with the triangle acting as a reversal pattern. The example used here also introduces the more difficult trading situation, in which there is actually a false breakout to complicate matters. The long trader who held his position until the completion of the pattern, if unwary, might have been fooled by the false upside breakout. There are, however, a number of warning signals. Remember, the breakout should occur well before the apex of the triangle is reached, which was not the case in our example. The volume of trading was also much too light to confirm the validity of the breakout. Rather than liquidating the position when the false breakout is suspected, the trader should find the minor bottom of the triangle which shows the greatest support, and place a sell stop order below it. This is usually the bottom with the highest volume. Since the pattern is so imperfect anyway, the trader should not expect any pullback once his protective stop at SS_7 is activated. Therefore, he may double up on his order there to initiate a short position. Of course, the triangle might also have experienced a nice clean downside breakout in the first place well before reaching the apex. Here, the trading tactics would have been greatly simplified. All long positions must be liquidated when the price closes below the confines of the triangle. Short positions may also be initiated at this point or on the possible pullback. Buy stops above a significant minor top of the triangle may be used.

Finally, triangle C represents the equally common triangle of consolidation within the downtrend. This time, the short seller has the odds in his favor. The stock will probably continue in the same direction after the pattern has been completed. Once again, good charting theory would require the trader to await completion of the formation before taking new short positions or liquidating long positions. Once the breakout occurs, any short sales may be protected with a buy stop order above the last minor top of the triangle at BS_2. Often, clues are given ahead of the breakout to warrant taking an early short position. One such clue is the failure of the stock to rally back up to the declining trendline of the triangle just before the downside breakout as in triangle C. The venturesome chartist who takes a position here should certainly protect it with a close buy stop at BS_2. After the breakout, the stop order may be moved to BS_3. The trader who wants to gamble that the triangle will be a reversal pattern and take a long position has the odds against him and should do nothing until the pattern is completed with a valid upside breakout.

RIGHT TRIANGLES

A considerable amount of space has been devoted to the discussion of the symmetrical triangle for two reasons. First, most of the description and trading tactics will also apply to all other triangles. Second, the symmetrical triangle is probably the pattern that the chartist will discover the most frequently in his trading. The reader will see in figure 8-2 that the shapes of the right triangles differ from the symmetrical only in that one of the connecting trendlines is horizontal. If the base of the triangle (the broad open end of the triangle) were drawn in, a right angle would exist in the triangle. This slight difference is, however, very important to the chartist. It demonstrates to him that both sides in the market are not of equal strength while the consolidation pattern is being formed. This, of course, gives the chartist advance indication of the eventual outcome of the struggle between buyers and sellers, and hence the direction of the move after the completion of the pattern. Almost everything else is similar to that of the symmetrical triangle. There are two types of right triangles, one that is inherently bullish and one that is bearish. Each will be considered separately.

ASCENDING RIGHT TRIANGLE

The ascending right triangle is the bullish pattern of the three triangle formations. Unlike the symmetrical triangle, a line drawn connecting the tops of each minor rally in this right triangle forms a straight *horizontal* line. Each minor rally is able to return to the same resistance point, while each intervening minor decline finds support at successively higher levels. The combination of trendlines, while still converging to form a triangle, definitely indicates that the balance of power is slightly in the hands of the buyers. The stock is still in an uptrend but it has temporarily run into a resistance point. The resistance may be one large order to sell or simply the resistance of a previous congestion area. Regardless of the source of the selling, it is evident that the stock is trying harder and harder to penetrate the resistance point, as indicated by the rising bottoms of the pattern. Eventually the selling is exhausted or orders are withdrawn, and the breakout will occur. This breakout is often a very strong one, for the actual point of completion is easy to pinpoint and there will be a large number of buy stop orders just above it. A well-formed ascending triangle will seldom fail to have an

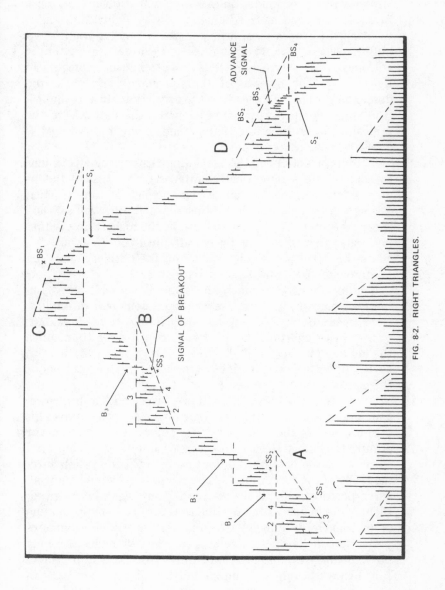

FIG. 8.2. RIGHT TRIANGLES.

upside breakout, and this upside breakout will seldom fail to supply a sizable move afterwards. The right triangle, while also a strong consolidation pattern, will probably act as a reversal formation more often than the symmetrical triangle. Even on these occasions, however, the ascending triangle is a bullish pattern, for when it does act as a reversal pattern it will invariably reverse a previous downtrend (see triangle A in figure 8-2). The reversal of the uptrend is left up to the descending right triangle. In either situation advance indication is given, since the implications of the pattern are the opposite to the direction of the trend in which it is found as a reversal pattern.

The construction of the ascending right triangle is similar to that of the symmetrical counterpart. The first of the required four minimum points is also the highest point reached during the triangle but, in this instance, all other rallies reach the same point. The volume is always the highest on the first peak and then gradually tapers off until the breakout. Because this breakout usually occurs on the upside, it must be accompanied by a very large increase in trading.

Trading tactics are much the same as those for the symmetrical pattern, but because of the obvious bullish implications, many chartists are tempted to anticipate the breakout. Conservative charting theory would still urge restraint until the actual completion of the formation. It would be helpful to lay down a few rules for coping with the temptations of this pattern.

First, the trader who finds himself with both a short position and an ascending right triangle might do well to cover his position before the breakout, since the odds so greatly favor an upside ending. He may protect his action by placing a sell stop below the pattern in order to reinstate his position automatically if the formation fails. A second rule would allow an early position only if an additional buy signal were given, such as the failure of the decline to return to the uptrend line as in triangle B. Finally, if the pattern nearly approximates perfection in its shape, size and volume characteristics, long positions may be instituted but only with close stop protection below the previous minor bottom. If these are successful, additional long positions may be added on the completion of the pattern, when the stock will finally break out and close beyond the resistance point of the top horizontal trendline. The volume characteristics and trading tactics of the pullback are exactly the same as in the symmetrical triangle.

DESCENDING RIGHT TRIANGLE

The descending right triangle has exactly the opposite implications and description as the ascending pattern. It is, of course, the bearish member of the triangle family, and is usually found within downtrends. Its pattern displays a top trendline connecting the minor tops of rallies within the pattern of a downward slanting line. It converges with the horizontal trendline which connects the minor bottoms of the intervening declines. The bearish implications of the pattern should now be evident at first glance in figure 8-2. It is clear from the chart that the stock is still in a downtrend even as it moves into a consolidation formation. Only the angle of descent changes. Looking at triangle D in figure 8-2, it can be seen that the decline has been temporarily halted by support, which this time may have come from a large *buy* order or a previous support area. The decline is still evident in the pattern, as each successive rally is a little weaker, while only the support forming the horizontal trendline stands in the way of the continuing trend downwards. Finally, the support is broken and the steeper decline is resumed. This is the usual picture of the descending triangle. Short positions can be taken on the breakout at S_2, with a stop above the last minor top at BS_3. If an advance signal is given as in triangle D, and early short position can be taken, with a stop above the previous minor top at BS_2.

Finally, triangle C is an example of the descending triangle when it acts as a reversal pattern. It will be found within an uptrend and should give the chartist plenty of advance warning.

RECTANGLES

DESCRIPTION

A consolidation formation very similar to the symmetrical triangle in everything except shape is the "rectangle." It is a congestion pattern which gives no advance indication as to the direction of the breakout. Also, as in the case of the symmetrical triangle, both buyers and sellers seem to be evenly matched throughout the formation of the pattern. However, instead of two converging trendlines as in the symmetrical triangle, the rectangle is formed by two parallel trendlines. The rectangles of figure 8-3 are representative of those to be found on most charts.

Usually, the lines connecting the minor tops and bottoms are horizontal. It is not uncommon, however, for the lines to remain parallel but also to slant. When the rectangle is slanting, the slant is almost always against the trend. That is, during an uptrend a falling rectangle will be found, while within a declining stock trend the lines will slant slightly upward.

Although the pattern displayed is generally a consolidation pattern, it may also serve as a reversal formation for either an uptrend or a downtrend. Since it may equally be a bearish or a bullish pattern, it must be watched very carefully, and breakouts must not be anticipated. The volume characteristics of the rectangle are also similar to that of the triangle, with the highest volume usually appearing at the beginning of the pattern and then gradually declining.

Looking at the two reversing rectangles of figure 8-3, it is not difficult to see why many chartist simply classify this pattern as something akin to the double top with an extra top or two. The implications are the same, whichever the classification. The important points to watch are the support area formed by the line connecting the minor bottoms of the fluctuations within the pattern and the resistance point supplied by the line connecting the minor tops. When either of the lines is penetrated, a move in that direction is signaled.

TRADING THE RECTANGLE

Because the rectangle pattern resembles several reversal patterns and also because it gives no advance indication of direction, it should be watched very closely. It is probably the most dangerous of the patterns mentioned up to this point. The trading procedure should be similar to that of the symmetrical triangle, with even more caution urged.

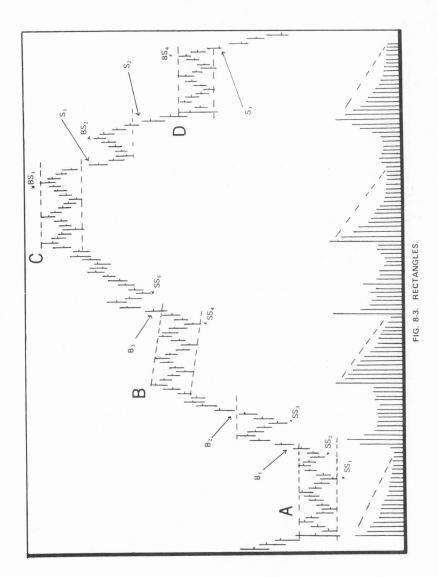

FIG. 8-3. RECTANGLES.

First of all, the breakout should definitely not be anticipated. Before taking a position based upon the breakout, care
should be taken to make sure that the pattern conforms to all
the conditions of validity. The volume should be low
throughout the formation. The upside breakout, to be valid,
should be accompanied with distinctly higher trading. Any
pullback following an upside breakout should not occur with
heavy selling but should be, instead, a very dull decline.

A long position, taken on an upside breakout as at B_1 or
B_3, should be protected with sell stop orders below the bottom trendline of the pattern, such as at SS_1 or SS_4. Anywhere along the move the chartist can, of course, take advantage of any minor bottoms to gradually move up his protective sell stop orders, as indicated in figure 8-3.

In triangles C and D, short sales are in order at S_1 and at
S_3, with protective buy stop orders at BS_1 or at BS_4 or at
any minor tops in between.

A FINAL NOTE ON THE MAJOR PATTERNS

The reader has now been exposed to most of the major
reversal and consolidation patterns. As he may now realize, it
is not always easy to separate them into neat categories. Consolidation patterns may, at times, become reversals and,
much less frequently, reversal formations might also represent only a rest. The list of patterns and variations of patterns
has by no means been exhausted. The formations represented
to this point are, by far, the most common and the most
reliable. A system based only upon these patterns, and
backed by a sound knowledge of support and resistance and
trendline analysis, would leave little lacking.

The patterns heretofore mentioned, however, usually
occur in the stocks that move up or down in a fairly orderly
manner. What of those wildly moving stocks which capture
the spotlight and seldom slow down even for short rests—
those stocks that capture the imagination of every trader,
new and old alike? The patterns mentioned to this point will
seldom appear on the charts of these stocks. There are some
additional charting phenomena, however, that apply particularly to this type of stock and offer some help to the trader.
They have been reserved for discussion in the next chapter.

Chapter 9

HIGH-VELOCITY STOCKS

In every bull market there are a number of industries and individual stocks that, because of their standout performances, gain most of the speculative publicity. Their sharp and rapid climbs excite the imagination of new traders and "old pros" alike with dreams of overnight success. They are the current "glamour stocks," that much later may be referred to by less endearing names. For the movements of these stocks are almost always overdone and are followed by sizable sell-offs. For some of them, the climb is well-grounded in fundamentals and although overdone, after the initial large correction they will resume their climb at a more sensible pace. Many others have no valid reason for the extent of their move, and traders who are caught at higher prices may never get even. Obviously, the risk is great and there is probably no trading situation that is more difficult to cope with. Ironically, it is also the situation in which there is the least amount of help available to the trader. The fundamentalist can certainly not tell him how far the emotionalism will eventually carry the stock before the fun is over. He is usually out of the position well before the fun begins. Charting and other technical tools are also less effective here but at least offer some aid. The reason for this lack is the obvious fact that the stock will seldom stop long enough to form meaningful support or resistance areas or any of the other recognizable patterns discussed to this point.

Yet, in spite of these problems, most traders are attracted to exactly this type of stock, as it offers the best chance for quick and substantial gains. As always, where the greatest profits lie, the most risk also abides and, quite naturally, the most losses. The trader who is wrong with such a stock is very wrong in terms of dollar losses. When the fun is over, the stock falls nearly as fast as it rose.

There is some hope for the trader, however, in charts. Although the rapid-moving stock seldom pauses for long, there are some chart formations or phenomena that are common to this type of stock. They have been grouped into this chapter in an attempt to bring some order into this phase of trading and to adapt chart trading especially to this type of stock.

FLAGS AND PENNANTS

The trader who decides to try for the fat profits offered by the high-velocity stock can certainly use any trading aids available. He must be suspicious of every minor pause in the forward progress of his stock, for this trend will be reversed just as quickly as it is moving. There will not usually be the broad reversal pattern at the end of the move, with its numerous warning signals. The consolidations, when they occur, will not resemble any of the patterns mentioned thus far. The most prevalent consolidation pattern found in the fast-moving stock is called the "flag" or "pennant," depending on the shape. The trading implications for both are the same, however.

THE FLAG

The reader already knows one characteristic of the flag: It is usually found only in rapidly moving stocks, since it is merely a short consolidation pattern that seldom lasts more than one month, and is often completed in a matter of days. The flag is not difficult to discover on the chart and, in fact, will stand out for the trader who is looking for it. There will, nevertheless, be many nervous moments while it is forming.

The short-term fluctuations of this small congestion area will form the shape of a small rectangle when the tops and bottoms are connected. It will slant against the trend, which is very steep. In fact, the move that immediately precedes the formation of the flag must be extremely sharp to qualify the pattern as an ideal flag. When the reader looks at the examples in figure 9-1, it is not difficult to see how the name of the formation evolved. When the two characteristics of shape and preceding move are taken together, the pattern looks exactly like a flag upon a flagpole.

The volume characteristics of the flag are of critical importance. The volume within the flag formation should stand out

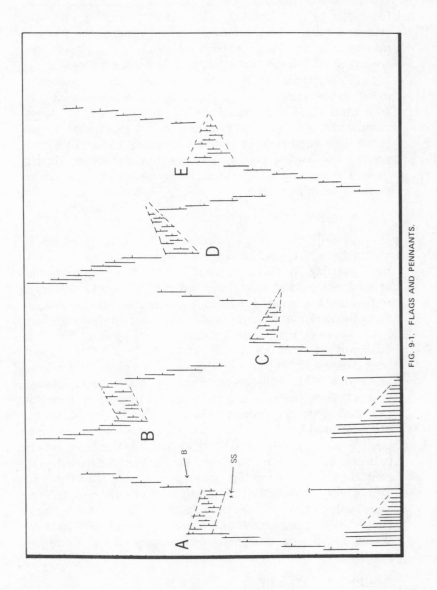

FIG. 9-1. FLAGS AND PENNANTS.

as a distinct contrast to the normally high volume of this type of stock, especially on the steep drive immediately preceding the formation of the pattern. The greater the contrast, the better or more valid the flag. Since the stock is making a temporary high, the volume at the beginning of the flag formation is quite high. As the pattern develops, however, the trading should drop precipitously. This sudden dullness in the typically dynamic stock is the best signal that the stock is merely undergoing light profit-taking and is not reversing. In fact, once the formation of the flag is suspected, any large-volume days within the flag should put the trader on his guard for a sudden reversal. For the pattern to be a complete success, the volume on the breakout from the pattern should show a drastic increase that causes the pattern completion to resemble an explosion.

THE PENNANT

It is hardly necessary to discuss the pennant separately. It differs from the flag formation only in the detail of shape. Like the flag, it slants downward within the uptrend and upward within a sharply declining trend. However, the lines connecting the minor tops and bottoms converge instead, to form the pennant shape in figure 9-1. An additional variation is the symmetrical pennant that does not slant at all. It is distinguished from the symmetrical triangle only by size and the existence of the flagpole.

At this point, the reader may be somewhat confused between these patterns and those of the triangles and rectangles studied in the previous chapter. This is, of course, an obvious question, since they are easily confused. Any mistake, however, is not too serious, as they are all consolidation patterns. It will be remembered that both the flag and pennant are small patterns that seldom take more than three to four weeks to form. The fluctuations within the patterns are also much smaller than in the patterns of the previous chapter. Finally, they are found only in the rapidly moving stocks, and the steep flagpole is a necessary part of the actual pattern.

TRADING PROCEDURE

Perhaps the most significant aspect of the flag and pennant

is the automatic measuring implications that they offer. When a valid flag or pennant is completed, the move that follows the breakout may be expected to carry as far as the sharp move that preceded it. Or, in other words, the flag or pennant may be thought of as the half-way point of a large move. This information obviously, can be extremely welcome to the trader. Before looking at exactly how this knowledge can be used, let us examine the breakout of this pattern more closely.

Because of the rapidity of the moves in a stock of this type, it is necessary to insist that the suspected pattern conform as closely to the ideal as possible. The straighter the flagpole and the greater the contrast between the trading volume before the flag, during the flag and on the breakout, the move valid is the pattern. Once the breakout occurs, with high volume, prices should move very rapidly away from the pattern. This move is often as steep as the flagpole preceding the pattern, and there is usually no pullback to the pattern. This breakout, because of the obvious risks, should not be anticipated.

Once all of the necessary conditions are met, a new long position may be taken and the previous long may breathe easier. A sell stop order may then be placed below the entire pattern for protection. The trader who was already long before the pattern formed could have protected himself with this same stop before the breakout occurred. To gage the minimum expected move following the breakout, the trader may measure the length of the flagpole from the beginning to the end, i.e., the top of the flag or pennant. This distance may then be projected from the breakout point. Although this approach may seem too mechanical to work, the well-formed flag and pennant is surprisingly consistent in gaining this minimum objective. Even the pattern that does not work is also an aid to the trader. He is at least left with a significant support area under which to place a stop order.

Although most of the above procedures referred only to the flag and pennant within the uptrend, they may be similarly applied to the rapidly declining stock. Even the volume characteristics are much the same. While the high-volume requirement on the upside breakout is not quite so important on the flag within the downtrend, it nevertheless is very common.

103

Another chart phenomenon common to the high-velocity stock which is at times very helpful to the trader is the trading "gap." The gap appears on the chart as a price area in which no trades occurred. It is most often caused by jump openings when, because of an overnight imbalance in buy or sell orders, the specialist in the stock is forced to open the stock at a price much higher or lower than the previous night's closing price. This would leave, in the case of the higher opening, a trading range for the day in which the low is much higher than the high of the range of the previous day, and therefore a gap appears on the chart. Any gaps that occur under these circumstances are usually quite informative to the trader in high-velocity stocks. Some gaps, however, are meaningless and they might better be quickly disposed of before beginning the discussion of the meaningful gaps.

First, there are many stocks whose average daily trading volume is extremely light. They are usually stocks that have a very small floating supply. Gaps, then, are very common occurrences to these stocks and relatively meaningless. Second, the reader has already learned that trading within most consolidation patterns is expected to be very low. Consequently, gaps occurring within the confines of such a pattern are also to be deemed as harmless. Finally, if the reader is familiar with the mechanics of the "ex-dividend" day, he knows that a stock usually opens lower on its ex-dividend day by the amount of the dividend. A gap caused, then, by a large stock or cash dividend is also of no value to the chartist. These three gaps have no technical meaning to the chartist. There are several instances, however, in which the gap is very important.

THE BREAKAWAY GAP

Many meaningful gaps occur as a stock is in the process of completing an important consolidation or reversal formation, or as it is breaking through a significant support or resistance area. A gap found in these circumstances, called a "breakaway gap," is often the forerunner of a high-velocity price move. It is also significant in a more orderly trading stock. Coming as it does, accompanying a breakout, it serves to

EXHAUSTION GAPS

MEASURING GAPS

BREAKWAY GAP

FIG. 9-2. GAPS.

confirm that breakout and should give the chartist much more confidence in the pattern. This gap is especially helpful when a chart pattern is a borderline case, that is, one that does not exactly meet all of the specifications of the perfect pattern. The presence of the gap may be the final evidence of the validity of the formation. In short, a breakout that occurs with a gap opening is considered more valid than one without. The appearance of the gap is also a good indication of the technical opinion of the charting community in general, since chartists are undoubtedly a major factor in the formation of the gap. A close slightly beyond the breakout point of a formation is often followed in the morning by chart buying and stop loss orders. The size of the gap is often good evidence of the possible force of the breakout. This type of gap is very common to breakouts from a flag or pennant and, to the conservative chartist, should be considered a prerequisite to a flag or pennant breakout. The breakaway gap, together with others to be mentioned, is pictured in figure 9-2.

THE MEASURING OR RUNAWAY GAP

The second appearance of gaps in the life of the high-velocity stock usually occurs at about the half-way point of the entire move. It is for this reason that these gaps are called "measuring gaps." While the breakaway gap usually occurs when there is little public attention focused upon the stock, the measuring gap appears when the stock is in full flower. At this time the trading volume is extremely high, and the popularity of the stock is growing. The news behind the movement, not usually known when the breakout occurs, has now been public for a short while and a large popular following is developing. The stock might have already appeared on the most active lists several times. It is here that the trading begins to get out of hand. The specialist is often forced, on many mornings, to mark up the price of the stock to satisfy the overnight accumulation of buy orders resulting in a number of gaps. The volatile nature of the trading during this period gives a second name to this gap—the "runaway" gap. It is probably at this time that many traders begin to feel that the move has been overdone, and the stock is beginning to

106

build a meaningful short position.

EXHAUSTION GAP

All good things must ultimately come to an end, and the stock market is no exception. The stock that formed gaps on its move up will usually form a few more shortly before the final top is made. These gaps are called "exhaustion gaps," and can be very valuable in predicting the top to the high-velocity stock. Trading is, once more, very erratic during this period. Contrary to the wild trading evident during the formation of the runaway gaps, however, the trading becomes more two-sided. Although the major trend may still be up, the astute tape-watcher will begin to notice that the short intra-day declines are becoming almost as large as the advances. Very often there are sharp rallies with light volume, caused by short-covering, followed by equally fast corrections with higher volume. The tape-watcher may also notice a number of large blocks on down-ticks that are disguised by the overall strength in the market.

Gaps are once again being formed as the specialist attempts to fill the overnight buy orders. Much of the buying, however, is done by short-sellers who shorted too early in the move and are either being "squeezed out" of their position by margin calls or simply giving up. The rallies are often very dramatic, but have little follow-through. For the first time in the lengthy move, a downside gap may appear as the trading becomes erratic. The specialist at these times has trouble matching the sell orders. After the final top is made, it is usually followed by several downside gaps.

Many beginners are concerned about the possibility of mistaking the exhaustion gap for the runaway gap. This is a very good question. However, the problem is not as difficult as may appear, as there are a number of ways to distinguish the two types of gaps. First, a stock usually tends to have the full set of gaps. If it has already had a set of runaway gaps earlier, the exhaustion gaps are to be expected. The volume during the period of the suspected exhaustion gaps is usually higher than that during the previous set of gaps. Trading volume tends to be higher at the final top in the move.

A second indication of the differences may be found in an examination of the action of the stock after the gap has been formed. Runaway gaps are usually followed by very strong market action, during which the price will move quickly and sharply up and away from the gap area. The force of the move will continue for several days before any corrections occur. In the exhaustion gap area, trading is much more erratic. The stock will have much more difficulty following through and often will not carry very far after the gap.

A third distinguishing characteristic of the runaway gap area is the existence of a flag or pennant. As the reader has learned, these consolidation formations are also found near the half-way point of the move, and are thus to be found in the same price area as the runaway gaps. On the other hand, if the gaps are found just as a previous flag's objective is being met, it is further evidence that they are exhaustion gaps.

Finally, look for evidences of excessive short-covering as a factor behind the movement. When much of the buying is done by short sellers, the stock is leaving little support beneath the move and is vulnerable to a sharp reversal. Gaps found in this type of atmosphere are almost certain to be exhaustion gaps.

ANATOMY OF A HIGH VELOCITY MOVE

As a method of summarizing what has been said in this chapter, we will trace the action that may occur in the history of a typical high-velocity stock. In terms of gaps, trading volume and flag or pennant formations, this history is usually found to be a three-phase movement. Follow now one of these moves from beginning to end.

PHASE I

Before any movement begins, there is always some preparation for the move which will appear on the chart. There is also, especially in the case of the dormant base, a slow build-up in trading volume. The move actually begins with the breakout from one of the patterns discussed. Accompanying the breakout is the high volume of the first phase, which is always necessary to validate the upside breakout. It is also here that the first of the gaps are found accompanying the breakout. The first gap is not usually "filled," that is, the stock will not subsequently sell back to trade within the gap area.

The first breakout and burst of volume usually occurs well before any news announcement is made of the fundamental reason for the move. This initial buying is first done by the insiders, followed by chartists and astute fundamental analysts. Shortly after the breakout, the news announcement that explains the activity is made. This occasions an even greater increase in volume for the first phase as traders react to the news. After the high volume of the breakout news announcement and the subsequent response to it are over, the high volume of the first phase gradually subsides to more normal volume as the stock continues to move higher.

PHASE II

The second burst of trading occurs about half way toward the end of the move. By this time, the public is becoming increasingly aware of the stock. There are frequent recommendations by advisory services, "write-ups" by leading brokerage firms and many articles in financial periodicals. It is in this phase that trading first begins to be unmanageable and one or several measuring gaps may occur. This phase is also identified by the formation of a flag or pennant, usually just before the heavier volume begins a peak. The gaps often accompany the completion of the consolidation formation. It is also in this phase that the short seller first becomes very active in the stock. As will be seen, it is this premature short-selling that provides much of the impetus for the final fling in the stock.

PHASE III

The third area of high volume and gaps is usually the last of the movement. The volume of this phase is usually the highest of the entire move, and is one of the identifying factors of this phase. It is during this final phase that most losses occur, for it is here that the most uninformed traders finally take their positions. The publicity of the stock is at its zenith and these traders, who probably do not usually trade in this type of stock, are finally enticed in. The trading in this

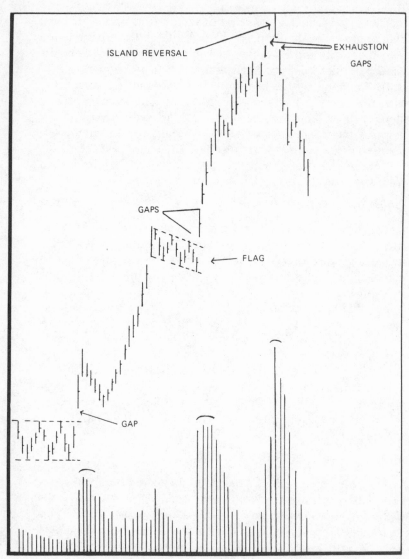

FIG. 9-3. THE THREE-PHASE HIGH-VELOCITY MOVE.

area is very hectic, and there is increasing evidence of high volume "churning," with the stock seemingly making little upward progress. Often, very strong upward daily moves tend to give up much of the gain by the close of day.

Much of the buying of this phase is supplied by disgruntled short sellers who are finally giving up. This type of buying is further evidence of the pending market top. Monthly short interest totals should begin to show declines in the stock. The existence of gaps is a further warning of the imminent disaster. Most of these upside exhaustion gaps are very quickly filled. Finally, the objectives of the flags or pennants of the second phase have probably already been met.

THE REVERSAL

The third and final phase of a high-velocity move naturally must end with a reversal of the trend and a sharp sell-off. This reversal will not, as mentioned earlier, resemble those of more moderately moving stocks. There is no broad and familiar reversal pattern to warn the trader, and there is not even significant support to warn him when it is broken. The end will be quick and disastrous for those left holding the "hot potato." The trading hints offered here should be very helpful if applied correctly, since they will tell the trader that he is in the general area of the reversal. If he is wise, he will not try for the exact top. Often, however, the exact top of the move will be signaled by another chart phenomenon common to the high-velocity stock. It is called the "one-day reversal" and, in its special form, the "island reversal."

THE ONE-DAY REVERSAL

At the top of the example of figure 9-3, the one-day reversal appears. The behavior of the stock on this day is outstanding. The price range is very wide for the day and the volume is usually the highest of the entire move. Although the stock pushes through to an all-time new high, the stock sells off to close at or near the low of the day. It is frequently making new lows for the day at the closing bell. The next morning will usually confirm the sudden reversal, with a large exhaustion gap caused by the flood of sell orders. It is this type of sudden death ending that oftens marks the end of high-

111

velocity stocks. If the other signals mentioned earlier are evident and the trader is faced with a one-day reversal, he is advised to liquidate immediately. A short position may be taken also, with a protective buy stop placed above the all-time high.

The action of the one-day reversal is quite dramatic, is easy to spot, and difficult to ignore. The same signal may be given, however, if the stock trades several days in a row with high volume and weak closings each day after wide price ranges and erratic trading.

THE ISLAND REVERSAL

When the one-day reversal is combined with exhaustion gaps in the manner depicted in figure 9-3, the chartist is given the most reliable reversal pattern for the high-velocity stock—the island reversal. The author has never seen one that was not followed by a substantial sell-off. As the reader can see, this pattern can hardly be missed. The one-day reversal is completely set apart from all other trading by gaps, leaving an island of trading. The existence of a gap caused by an excess of buy orders, followed by a new high, and then followed by a gap caused by excessive selling illustrates the force of the reversal. The frenzied trading is very often a sign of the top. The island reversal has as its minimum objective the reversal of the entire preceding sharp rally which, in the case of the high-velocity stock, is frequently the majority of the move.

CONCLUSIONS

The high-velocity stock, as mentioned, is the most difficult of all to trade. This is naturally the case, since because the prospect of reward is high, the risk is correspondingly high. Because the move in this type of stock is dominated by emotional speculation, fundamental analysis is of little use. Charts, though not as helpful as usual, do offer the only real aid. The tools mentioned in this chapter will help. With luck and the use of timely stop orders where significant support areas occur, the prospects of success are enhanced appreciably.

112

A FINAL WORD ON CHARTING PRINCIPLES

The reader has now been introduced to the basic principles of charting and technical analysis of individual stocks. Although this encounter has been brief in comparison to other charting texts, none of the basic concepts of this approach to stock analysis have been omitted. Many of the minor details of technical analysis have been bypassed, in an effort to avoid excessive detail at the expense of the important concepts. Charting is a highly individualistic art, and the missing details can best be acquired through experience.

The word experience is stressed because the beginner will very quickly find that his trading will not always be confined to perfect textbook patterns. If he waits for the perfect patterns he will miss out on many exciting trades. Most of the benefits of charting will, instead, accrue to the chartist through his everyday exposure to support and resistance areas, borderline patterns and proper placement of stop orders. He will find many variations of the basic patterns mentioned in this text. With the arsenal of formations the reader has acquired, he should be ready to cope with any situation.

But there is another and more compelling reason why the author has purposely omitted many details of technical analysis, such as the more exotic chart constructions like "point and figure" charts, "moving averages" and the myriad sophisticated variations of the simple concepts already expounded. The purpose of this book is to make the reader a successful trader, *not* merely a "chartist." After he is strongly in possession of these basic concepts and has worked with charts, the trader will find them a very helpful tool. But he should use this new tool in a creative manner with his other knowledge. Every trader, as mentioned earlier, is looking for the perfect "gimmick." The author does not want to be guilty of supplying what looks like one, since there is no one system that eliminates any need for further thinking. However, many of the pseudoscientific charting systems would lead the reader to believe just that.

It is hoped that by now the reader has a firm understanding of the broad framework of charting and is sold on its merits as a short-term trading aid. The trader who attempts to profit from short-term price swings without these principles in mind is not a complete trader and is doomed to failure. After working with charts, the trader should eventually arrive at the state of mind where he would not dream of taking a position in a stock without first examining a chart of that stock. To do otherwise is to approach the trade blindly. Once these habits are formed, he is ready to use charts to advantage.

The most important point of all to remember is that charts are only one of many tools that are not only helpful but necessary to success in trading. The more working tools that can be included in an orderly approach to trading, the better will be the chances of success.

In the final section, the use of charts will be fully integrated into a broad trading scheme. Many of the important principles and refinements of charting have been saved for this section, where their introduction will make more sense within the framework of the final trading system.

SECTION III

Trading Tactics

Chapter 10

THE BEST OF ALL POSSIBLE WORLDS

This section begins where altogether too many charting texts leave off. Although they may adequately present the theory of charting, they fail in teaching its application. This costly lesson is taught the beginner somewhere between his exposure to the principles of charting and his learning to profit from them. It is here that he incurs the large losses that may impel him to forgo technical analysis long before it has been given a fair chance. He is led to believe that, by some wonderful magic, he may directly transform the written word to large profits with little effort on his part in between. It is the purpose of this book to fill this void.

In the chapters ahead, the principles the reader has already learned will be refined further. He will be shown how to take the important step from theory to practice without losses. Using these refined principles, a broad trading system will be developed that he may use for everyday trading and, best of all, it is a system that will show immediate improvement in his trading results.

An important point to remember is that it is neither necessary nor desirable to throw away the knowledge that has already been accumulated. Too often, the beginning chartist completely scraps everything he has learned when he begins his new approach. Instead, he should avoid the trap of classifying himself as either a technician or a fundamentalist. Wherever possible, new tools should be blended into whatever system of analysis and trading is already being used. If the trader's fundamental analysis is faulty, it should be improved, not traded for some new tool. The system that includes the most tools, utilizing the best of each, is the system that is most likely to yield good results. As the trader becomes more proficient with all the tools, he must then gradually decide which to give the most weight in his decisions.

This final section will be aimed at the task of gradually

blending this newly learned technical approach into the reader's present fundamental approach to the market. While continuing to use fundamental analysis for all basic decisions, the reader will be taught how to gradually blend in first, the basic concepts of support and resistance and finally, the remaining principles. By maintaining his previous approach and improving it only gradually with technical analysis, he can certainly avoid the early losses usually suffered by the beginner. The final aim of this section is to take as much of the risk as possible out of short-term trading and to develop a well-coordinated system combining the best of both approaches, leaving room for any other helpful tools.

While the "true chartist" would object vehemently to this mixture, the reader must keep in mind that charts tell only the short-term balance of supply and demand for the stock. If the chart is not accurately read or if it simply gives a false signal, the trader must then examine what he is left with. Too often, in the excitement of the technical pattern, a position is taken in a stock which even the most perfunctory fundamental analysis would reject.

This voyage from purely theoretical exposure to charts to their practical application may be accomplished in a broad three-step approach, with only a few detours for additional refinements. In the first step, the reader will use a very simple system based upon his original fundamental approach but which also will introduce the basic concepts of support and resistance. During this phase, he will begin to construct charts, look for support and resistance areas and, finally, utilize them for setting objectives and for placing stop orders, all the while making most decisions on the basis of fundamental considerations.

After a suitable period of introduction, the reader will be ready for the second stop. Still selecting his stocks on the basis of fundamentals, he will then begin to make increasing use of formations to decide which of his fundamental selections are ready for trading positions. Many readers who do not intend to engage in extreme short-term trading and want to maintain the major emphasis on fundamental analysis may stop here, refine both approaches and have a fine system of trading.

Those readers intent on trading the extreme short-term price swings, however, must be prepared to place increasing emphasis upon charting. They must take the third step, in which all trading positions are taken on the strength of chart patterns. But even in this more advanced technical system, fundamental analysis will be utilized.

Following these three steps, even further refinements will be made in the interests of more profitable trading. A chapter will be devoted to an in-depth analysis of the breakout, the most critical point of charting.

Finally, to this fully refined charting-based system of trading will be added the most neglected ingredient of successful trading . . . psychology. It has often been said that the good trader is able to trade any commodity equally well. Although every field requires a certain technical expertise, there are certain other factors that are common to all traders who make good. These factors are something beyond the mechanics of trading, and include such obvious factors as objectivity, the proper mental attitude and other psychological preparations. The most important of these that are pertinent to stock trading will be discussed and included in the final system of trading.

Chapter 11

BREAKING THE ICE

Now that the reader has been introduced to technical analysis, the next question is how can it best be employed in actual short-term trading. As mentioned earlier, the tendency of most beginners is to drop completely their previous trading habits and knowledge and to plunge directly into their new panacea. The abrupt change and over-enthusiasm usually leads to disappointment, losses and finally abandonment of charting before it is truly learned. What, then, is the most painless and least expensive way to begin to profit from charts? The answer is that it should be a method that involves the least amount of initial change in the usual system of trading.

If the reader is like most traders, he has no real system at all. Since most of his decisions are based upon some form of fundamental analysis, it is indeed difficult to establish any system, for there is little connection between the fundamentals and short-term price swings. At times, he may perform as complete a fundamental analysis of his stock as he is capable of. He will study statements, annual reports and learn as much of the company as possible. Much more frequently, however, his analysis is much less penetrating. Often, he will take a position solely upon the basis of a favorable recommendation by a brokerage firm or advisory service. On other occasions, he will act solely on tips or rumors, with little or no study. In any case, once his position is taken he has little idea as to when he will take his profit should he earn one. Nor does he have any notion of how long he will hold his position, especially if he should incur a loss. (Charts, of course, are most helpful here.) Finally, he is probably also trying his hand at the difficult game of trading the business news.

If he has been trading for a long while, whether his analysis and results are good or bad, he has probably learned many things about the market. He has probably also lost some of his capital learning many things the hard way. He should not let all of this effort be wasted. It is not the purpose of this book to substitute one method of trading for another, but rather to add something of value to the general skills of the trader. Although it is not in the scope of this book to improve the reader's skills in fundamental analysis, it nevertheless assumes that he has some and that he will strive to improve them even as he is learning to apply charting skills.

INTRODUCING THE CHART

This chapter will introduce to the reader a very effective, yet simple, system that combines only the principles of support and resistance with his present fundamental approach. Many experienced chartists, in fact, prefer a simple system of this type to one that utilizes the more advanced trading theories. With this system the decisions as to which stocks to trade will still be made strictly on fundamental considerations. In this way, the reader will make no major changes at the outset. He may first introduce charts into his trading system by constructing charts of stocks that are attractive to him on a fundamental basis. He should then try to form the habit of always consulting his chart before making any trading commitment and to continue to study it while the position is maintained. In this way, he will become familiar with chart performance while he is still trading on a completely fundamental basis. Once this has been practiced for a suitable length of time, he may then begin to utilize support and resistance areas in the manner to be explained in this chapter.

The addition of the analysis of support and resistance areas to a trading system will improve results in several ways: First, the timing of commitments can be improved immediately. Second, once the position has been taken, profit objectives may be set much more effectively. Finally, stop loss orders may now be placed in a much more logical manner. In short, the introduction of charts will immediately improve the most critical areas of short-term trading: When to get in, how much profit to expect in the short term, when to get out and, finally, where stop orders may be placed.

OBJECTIVES

One of the first problems of the short-term trader that can be alleviated through the use of charts is that of setting price "objectives." This widely used technical term simply refers to the distance that the stock may be expected to travel in the short term. The discussion of this particular aspect of charting has been saved until now so that it may be covered in greater detail. It will be discussed once again in conjunction with pattern analysis in later chapters.

In this first simple system, however, the reader will learn to set short-term price objectives by using only the theories of support and resistance. This can be done even though the original commitments are made on a purely fundamental basis. Fundamental analysis can tell the trader what any stock should be selling for, but it cannot tell him when the market will begin to move it. When the stock is rising, fundamental analysis cannot tell the trader where it will stop in the short term. For these reasons, the trader should use charts to aid in setting goals for the days or weeks ahead. There are two different methods of finding objectives for planned trades when using only the notions of support and resistance.

THE COUNT

The first method, called the "count," is a term coined by "point and figure" chartists, but is one which may also be used with the simple bar chart. To understand this method, it is necessary to recall the earlier discussion of congestion areas. Each time that a stock pauses in its primary movement for a sideways congestion area, something very meaningful is happening. The longer that the stock continues to trade within a sideways pattern, the greater are the number of old positions that are liquidated and new ones that are replacing them. The longer the congestion pattern endures, the greater will be the proportion of new trading positions in which there is neither a profit or a loss of any magnitude. There are many new traders with long positions and also some with new short positions. When the pattern is inevitably completed and the breakout occurs, one of these groups will suddenly find itself with a loss. Many of these traders in the group protected themselves with stop orders which are touched off on the breakout, and others are ready to take a quick loss while it is still small. Consequently, any breakout is accentuated by this loss-taking, whether by the long traders or by those who are short. This, of course, is the reason for the sharp move that usually follows a breakout from a congestion area. Add to this moving force all the new positions that are taken by traders because of the breakout, and a dynamic move can be expected. The greater the number of traders involved, the greater will be the impetus behind the breakout move. In fact, the method of the "count" presumes a direct one-to-one relationship between the length of the congestion pattern and the length of the vertical move that follows the breakout. This, then, is the first objective relationship to be learned from this simple system of support and resistance. *The trader may expect that a stock, following its breakout from a congestion area, will continue its move for at least the distance that it traveled sideways during the formation of the congestion area.* Although it is difficult to say that such a perfect one-to-one relationship does exist, it is easy to see that a relationship of some type exists and, from the foregoing, it should not be difficult to understand the reason. The reader may resolve any doubts by simply glancing at a number of charts. He will see that a rapid move almost always follows the completion of a congestion pattern. He will also see that the larger congestion areas will usually be followed by the longest moves.

CONGESTION AREAS AS OBJECTIVES

A second, and perhaps more accurate method of finding objectives, is the position of the congestion areas themselves. This method involves the use of past congestion areas as near term price objectives. For the long position, the near term objective should be the next significant resistance area above the market price of the stock. If a short position has been taken, the near term objective lies below the market at the next support area. If the nearby objective is then penetrated, succeeding support or resistance areas may be used to find the next objectives. It is, more or less, a method of taking advantage of the sharp moves between congestion areas. Let us now see how these two approaches may be worked into the simple trading system.

TRADING THE RISING MARKET

Before illustrating this combined system of trading, it would be wise to review the ground rules. First, all major

123

decisions regarding which stocks to trade will still be made upon sound fundamental analysis. Stocks selected for long positions should be those in good financial condition, with opportunities for growth either in the long or intermediate term. The trader, however, is interested in trading only for the short-term. That is, he is interested in holding the stock only so long as the trend continues in his favor over the short term. When the trend turns, regardless of the long-term fundamental prospects, he wishes to liquidate. He will then look for another stock with short-term possibilities. The use of charts will enhance his chances to do just that.

In this first illustration, a long commitment has already been made solely upon fundamental considerations, but the chartist is interested only in the short-term objective. Later, the timing of the original commitment using support and resistance analysis will be discussed.

SETTING THE OBJECTIVE

Once the commitment is made, the trader may consult the chart in a search for all significant resistance areas above the market and all support areas below the market. This was the congestion area from which the stock has most recently broken out of. Applying the principle of the count, a rough notion of the potential move may be computed. The length of the ensuing move will, it may be recalled, be dependent upon the length of the sideways movement. More important, however, is the next resistance area above the market.

Naturally, the chart must be long enough to enable the trader to look back to see the resistance that was formed on the previous decline. As the reader may see from the chart in figure 11-1, the stock has left a number of resistance areas in the previous downtrend. This second method is by far the most important, particularly when significant resistance areas do exist. If the stock is moving into new high ground, then only the count is available to aid in setting an objective. A combination of both methods should be used whenever possible for, as always, the more tools used, the better.

If, for example, the count uncovers one objective but there is a strong resistance area at a point before the count objective is reached, the resistance area must be taken as the next

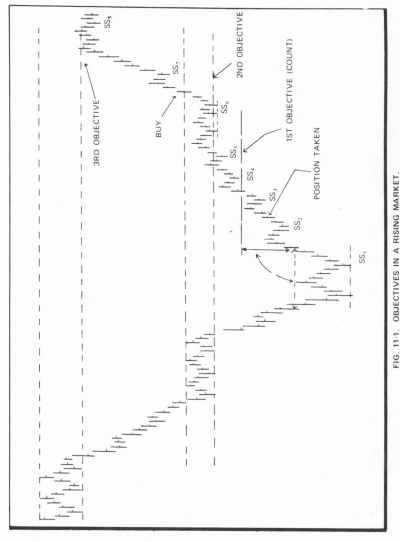

FIG. 11-1. OBJECTIVES IN A RISING MARKET.

objective. If, on the other hand, the count objective would be reached before the next resistance area, both may be used for objectives. The resistance area must be retained as the primary objective, since it is a more valid method, but caution should be exerted at the price area at which the count objective is reached, since a possible reversal may materialize at that point before the resistance area is even reached.

WHEN THE OBJECTIVE IS REACHED

As long as the stock continues to progress toward the objectives set by the chartist, he should continue to hold his long position. If a short-term trendline is formed during the course of the move, stop orders may be used for protection in the manner described in Chapter 6. Once the resistance area is reached, however, the trader should immediately be on guard for a possible reversal. As the stock begins to churn in its efforts to penetrate the resistance, the chartist should watch very closely for changing supply and demand relationships. In other words, he seeks to discover who is winning the battle, the disgusted sellers who form the resistance area or the buyers who have moved the stock up to the resistance area. Until the trader has a clear idea of the answer to this question, he must hold his position. There are a number of important clues that may be given as to the outcome of the struggle if the chart is examined closely enough. Some of these are demonstrated in figure 11-1.

One such clue is given in the character of the minor rallies and declines. If the stock rallies frequently into the resistance area but each intervening decline backs the stock off only slightly, it is a good sign that the primary trend is still intact. A second clue lies in the volume during each of these minor turns. If the volume remains high or steadily increases on each of the rallies, while remaining light or decreasing on each of the declines, it is a good indication that the resistance area will eventually be penetrated and that the position should be held. A third advance indication of a possible breakthrough is given by the distance that the rally is able to penetrate the resistance area. On the initial encounter with the resistance, if the rally is able to penetrate deeply into the area before being thrown back for the first time, it has a good chance at ultimate success. Those rallies that continue to be repulsed at the lower limits of the resistance area are usually the ones that will finally turn down and fail to penetrate. This, however, can only be a rough estimate until the chartist has studied the resistance area in depth in an attempt to pinpoint the strongest resistance price within the pattern. If he is able to pinpoint the most significant resistance price as being at the lower limits of the pattern, for example, then the analysis above may be slightly in error. Once the trader can pinpoint the selling potential within the pattern, his job is much easier. If, for another example, this significant point is in the middle of the entire area, once it is penetrated the chartist may not wish to wait until the entire area has been penetrated before liquidating.

One of the clearest signs of a failure of the move to break-out and thus, a reversal, is a sudden sharp sell-off, often with an acceleration in trading. It is most apparent when the stock has labored for a number of days or weeks to break through and the trading has become very dull. The sharp contrast of higher volume and a precipitous decline looks exactly as if the buyers had all decided to give up all at once.

Frequently, the trader may protect himself from this sudden surrender. Very often, the declines following each attempt to rally will find support at some common price on the chart. If the point has been tested several times, it is good trading practice to place a stop order just below this point as at SS_6 in figure 11-1. The trader may then watch the battle, while being protected from a sudden sell-off on the penetration of this minor support price, which would indicate that the sellers had taken the upper hand.

After the reader has had considerable experience with this system, he will begin to distinguish other clues which are helpful in trading these congestion areas. In summary, once the objective area is reached, the stock should be watched carefully but given every chance to break through. No move should be taken until a clear signal is given.

A CONSERVATIVE APPROACH

There is another, more conservative policy that is followed by many traders. As soon as the objective congestion area is attained, the trader will immediately liquidate his position, particularly if the stock is facing a very formidable resistance area. He may still observe the stock closely but probably more objectively, since he does not have a position at this crucial time. Once a breakthrough is made, he may re-establish his long position or he might even double his original position to make up for the few points that he missed because of his caution. In either case, a few points may be considered as cheap insurance against a sudden reversal.

Another variation to this same approach involves the use of stop orders. The trader still liquidates his position as soon as the resistance area is reached but he will, in addition, place an open buy stop order just above the top of the resistance area. In this way, he can install even move objectivity into his trading. He has automatically decided to liquidate his position when the resistance is reached and also to reinstate it if the area is breached. There is no room for changing his mind. If, on the other hand, the stock fails to penetrate the resistance area, he is safe from the decline and might even take a short-term short position. The short position could very effectively be protected by a buy stop order, placed just above the resistance area that so successfully withstood the onslaught of the uptrend.

In this simple system which combines both the fundamental and technical considerations, the trader may decide between this more conservative approach and the one mentioned earlier. Perhaps his opinion of the fundamental strength of the stock should be the deciding factor.

THE BREAKTHROUGH

When the breakout finally occurs, the trading tactics are much simpler. If the long position was held throughout the struggle, the trader may now prepare for the next objective. If the breakout occurs with high volume, as it should, he may even add to his previous position. If the position was liquidated prior to the breakout, a new one may now be taken. This would be especially good policy if the next objective portends a move of considerable proportions. Both the new positions and the ones previously taken should now be protected with a sell stop order placed just below the resistance area that was just penetrated. This now becomes a significant support area. The protective stop is even more important if the breakout was not accompanied by significant volume.

Now the trader is ready to look ahead to additional profits, protected by the stop order. He will set his next objective in the same way that he set his previous one. The next significant resistance area above the market should be the prime objective. Use may also be made of the count, especially if the breakout has taken the stock into new high ground. The position will be held until the objective is reached, at which time the trader may again follow either of the two policies explained above.

A BEAR IN A BULL MARKET

Suppose now that the situation is not quite so pleasant, and the trader finds himself with a short position just as a resistance area is approached. A rising market means only losses for the short seller, but this is exactly the wrong time to finally take a trading loss. Since the stock is now facing a serious threat to its further upward progress. the short seller would be wiser to lose a few more points as insurance against covering just as the market is turning down.

Instead, the trader may immediately place a buy stop slightly above the resistance area or, if he is able to pinpoint the most significant resistance point within the area, a stop just above that price. He may now wait objectively for the test of the resistance area as he lets the market make up his mind for him. He will be looking for the same clues of a possible reversal that were discussed above. If there are enough clues to a possible reversal, he might add to his short position with the same protective stop order, since if the stock fails to break through, he will be in a better position to make up any previous losses. Unlike the long trader, he would not, of course, follow the more conservative approach of liquidating as soon as the resistance area is reached. If the breakthrough finally occurs, he will be automatically liquidated by his stop orders.

TRADING THE DECLINING MARKET

The alert trader should, of course, always be searching for

candidates for short sales as well as the healthier companies. If the overall market is declining he should, indeed, be concentrating his efforts on those stocks that might be expected to fall even faster than the market. Too often, the trader who has been successful in trading the market from the long side during its rising phase gives back all of his profits by trying to find those few stocks that will rise against the falling market. If he is not prepared to use the short sale as a trading tool, he should at least find the discipline to stay on the sidelines until the market conditions are more favorable. The same simple dual system used for long positions can also be equally successful as a system for the short seller. Once again, it is assumed that the short position is taken for fundamental reasons and that the trader is interested in charts for trading guidelines. Much of the procedure previously explained can be applied to trading from the short side.

SETTING OBJECTIVES

Once again, the trader who has taken a position can derive two very important points of information from his chart. He may immediately find a significant price for a protective stop order. Once his position is protected, he may then use the chart to set his near term price objective. Looking at figure 11-2, the reader will see that much of this trading procedure is merely the reverse of that previously discussed for the long commitment. In the example, a short position was taken shortly after the pullback to the reversal pattern failed. The trader has two important points for stop orders immediately presented to him. He might first place his protective buy stop order slightly above the resistance of the reversal pattern at BS_1. Later, after the stock has moved lower, he may lower his stop order to a point just above the high price of the pullback at BS_2.

Once having placed his stop order, the trader is then free to concentrate on his profits. By measuring across the sideways movement of the previous reversal pattern, this count may be projected downward from the breakout point as the first objective. The second and more effective objective is found at the last significant congestion area below the market. Unlike the trading tactics previously explained, the

130

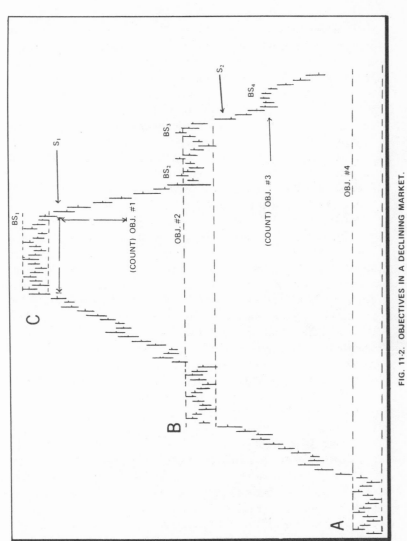

FIG. 11-2. OBJECTIVES IN A DECLINING MARKET.

trader is now looking for support from this area. The second objective is then set at the price that marks the top of support area B.

WHEN THE OBJECTIVE IS REACHED

There are again two general trading schemes to apply when the objective is reached, depending upon the faith the trader has in his fundamental analysis. First, the trader may decide to remain with his short position until the support area is penetrated or until some definite signal is given that the area will halt the decline. Many of the same clues mentioned earlier will also be of aid to the short seller in assessing the potential strength of the support area.

If the first several declines penetrate deep into the area of support, the trader should feel somewhat relieved, since he is now short. The decline that finds substantial support at the very top of the area is much more to be feared.

Each rally and decline during the test of the support area will give the same helpful information that was previously mentioned. If each rally is unable to move very far from the support area and can garner little trading volume behind it, then the support area is unlikely to hold. If the support is going to hold, the rallies usually become stronger each time the stock completes a successful test of the support area. The volume often increases on each new rally, as the stock is gradually building a base for an extended advance. If these rallies, in either case, make minor tops at one specific price area, the position may be protected with a buy stop order just above this point, as in BS_3 in figure 11-2.

The other general trading scheme, a conservative one, is to immediately liquidate the short position as soon as the support area is approached. A sell stop order may be immediately placed below the support area to reinstate the position if the support is penetrated. Once more, if the trader is able to pinpoint the most significant price within the support area, the sell stop may be placed much closer to the top of the support area without waiting for the stock to break down below the entire area before reinstating the position.

THE BREAKOUT

Once the support area has been successfully penetrated, new short positions may be taken and others reinstated. All positions taken should be protected immediately by the placement of a buy stop order slightly above the penetrated support area at BS_3, which is now an area of resistance to any further rally. Although accelerated trading frequently accompanies this downside penetration, its presence is not necessary to confirm it. Any pullback following the breakout may be used for further short selling if the volume on the rally is very light. Once all positions are taken and protected with appropriate stop orders, the entire procedure of selection of objectives is repeated.

A BULL IN A BEAR MARKET

It has been shown that charts can be very helpful in a declining market to the short seller. But what of the unfortunate long trader who is on the wrong side of this decline? How can the charts help him? His situation is, of course, analogous to that of the short seller in the rising market that was examined earlier. He is obviously wrong, but how does he decide just when to throw in the towel? Before any trader takes his loss, he should always take at least one quick look at a chart of his unfortunate selection. The vast majority of all reversals occur at a support or a resistance area. It is the increasing buying or selling of these areas that finally manage to turn the trend. If the trader finds that the stock is very near an important support area, he is certainly advised to await the outcome of the battle since it may just be that the reversal is near.

The best procedure would probably be to immediately place a sell stop order below the suspected support area. This would take him out of his position once the area is penetrated, and would remove the temptation of liquidating a little early. As always, charts may be used simply as a psychological aid. The trader may then watch and study the attempts of the stock to penetrate the support area. Whenever a number of signals are given that the support area will hold, the trader may then add to his long position to average down his price. All positions may still be protected with a stop order just below the support area.

TIMING THE NEW COMMITMENT

Up to this point in the development of this system of trading, it has been assumed that each original commitment was made solely upon fundamental considerations and that the chart was introduced only after the position was already taken. It was shown how helpful chart analysis could be in setting short-term profit goals, protecting the position with well-placed stop orders based upon support and resistance points and liquidating the position at the proper time. Now this system will be expanded to add one more important use for charts—refining the timing of the original commitment, whether long or short. With this expansion, the system will be complete, spanning the entire trade from beginning to end. The use of stop orders in initiating new positions will also be examined in depth. Since charts will be used to sharpen the timing of each commitment, a method must also be found to enable the trader to actually place the order at the proper time. Since most traders are not able to watch the market closely enough to do this, the stop order can be made to take his place.

TIMING THE PURCHASE

Remember that we have assumed in this first introductory trading system that all decisions to purchase were based upon an analysis of the fundamental conditions of the company. Since this decision did not consider market conditions when the actual purchase is to be made, the trader may find his stock in any of a number of situations when he is ready to take his position. With the aid of the chart, he may select the most favorable circumstances under which to make the purchase. (See figure 11-3.)

IN A RISING MARKET

It is always easy for the trader to reconcile the fact that the stock he selected for purchase is rising. But when does he buy it? Does he make his purchase immediately or does he

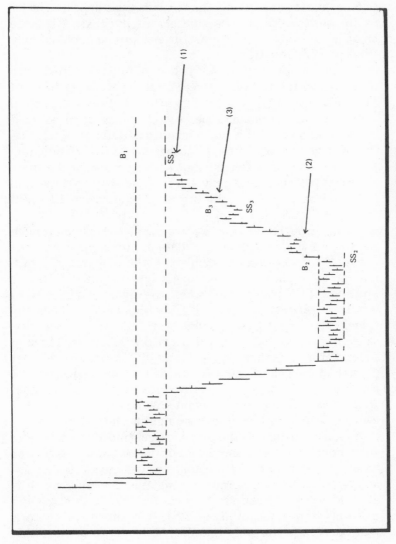

FIG. 11-3. TIMING THE PURCHASE IN A RISING MARKET.

wait for a dip in the market? If he buys after a strong rally, which is then followed by a technical correction in the price, how much of a short-term loss can he suffer? These are the common questions of timing that the average trader asks himself no matter how strong the fundamentals appear. This is, of course, the cue for the entrance of the chart. When the chart is consulted, it will show the stock to be in one of only three possible situations.

(1) The stock may be just below an important resistance area ((1) in figure 11-3). Here, the obvious answer to all of his questions is to wait. Using all of the hints and clues given earlier, he must wait until the obstacle has been surmounted (B-1), or at least until he has a number of definite signals that this will be accomplished. If he has a number of potential purchases that he is following or he cannot watch the stock carefully, the purchase may be initiated with a buy stop order placed just above the breakout point from the resistance area (figure 11-3).

This is probably as good a place as any to stop to examine the uses of the stop order to initiate positions. As mentioned above, the stop order is very helpful when the trader is waiting for a number of stocks to get into the proper trading position. It is also helpful when the trader is not able to watch the market as carefully as he should. Too often, the trader will correctly analyze his chart but, through an oversight, neglects to take the position at the right time. The stop order naturally solves this problem by having the delayed market order placed just as soon as the correct position of the breakout is determined. The trader is not only relieved from watching for the breakout but his order is executed even more quickly than if he were right in the boardroom.

As a further hint to the proper placement of this initiating stop order, the reader should recall the earlier discussions of natural support and resistance at even numbers. If, for example, the trader determines that the breakout point is 19 1/4, he should consider the natural resistance at 20 and place his stop order to buy at 20 1/4. In this way, the stock must penetrate not only the upper boundaries of the resistance but also the whole number resistance before the stop order will be activated. The stop order must be placed at such a significant point that if it is penetrated, there is little doubt in the mind of the trader that the move will continue. The double precaution of the breakout point and the natural resistance is particularly necessary when an initiating stop order is used because there is no assurance at the time that the stop is activated that the stock will *close* beyond the breakout point. Most conservative charting theory calls for not only a penetration but also a close beyond the breakout area.

(2) A second possibility confronting the trader is a situation in which the stock has only recently broken through a resistance area and which, therefore, has a support area immediately below ((2) in figure 11-3). This is probably one of the most favorable situations that the trader might face. He may take his long position without delay (B_2), while placing a protective stop order below the support area (SS_2). He may then look to an objective in the vicinity of the next resistance area above the market or he may use the count technique applied to the congestion area immediately below the market.

(3) The third and final possibility facing the trader is the most difficult to trade. It is the situation in which the stock is found to be equidistant from either an important support area or an overhanging resistance area ((3) in figure 11-3. The first problem that arises is the placement of a protective stop order. A stop order below the previous support area would risk a loss too great for the average short-term trader. A position would then be without stop protection unless there were minor bottoms (SS_3) or other small congestion areas suitable for a close stop order. Without these a position should only be taken if the trader is firmly convinced of the basic fundamental condition of the company and could endure a move all the way down to the previous support area without panicking. Indeed, the trader might better wait for better timing on this stock or abandon it for another.

IN A DECLINING MARKET

For the trader attempting to take a long position in a declining market, an entirely new set of problems arises. The big question is: Where is the bottom? A great deal of money is lost in the stock market by traders who are guessing at the

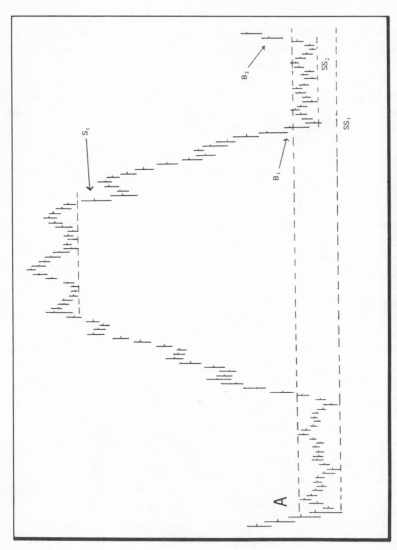

FIG. 11-4. TIMING THE PURCHASE IN A DECLINING MARKET.

bottom. Each sizable sell-off brings in a new rash of bargain-hunters who find that there are greater bargains later. The answer is to let the chart tell you when the bottom has been reached. The odds are very much in favor of the bottom materializing at a previous congestion. Therefore, the trader's procedure is simply to find out which support area will stem the decline.

If the stock has just broken an important support level (as at S_1 in figure 11-4) when the trader first consults the chart, he should obviously wait. He should also look for the next significant support area below the market (Congestion Area A) and bide his time waiting for the test. Once the support level is reached, he may take a position depending on several factors.

If the support area is very narrow, he may take a position (B_1) immediately just above the upper limits of the area, and protect his position with a stop order directly below the lower limits of the area. If, on the other hand, the support area encompasses a wide trading range, the tactics must change somewhat. A purchase above the upper limits with a stop below would entail an excessive potential loss. Therefore, a more detailed investigation must be made into the support area, in an effort to uncover the most important support price within the broad trading range. A purchase may then be made at a price slightly above this point, if one can be isolated, and a stop order placed below.

A final tactic, perhaps more conservative, is to avoid a position until the support area has been successfully tested and a new broad advance has started. The disadvantage to this tactic is the problem of deciding just when the test has been completed. That is, how far the rally must continue up from the support are before it is considered to have passed the test. This, of course, requires giving up a large amount of the potential profit of the rally in order to be sure. The advantage of the first tactic is that a position is taken very near what may turn out to be the bottom and if the trader is wrong, he will suffer only a small loss since he has stop order protection. He then has his funds free to try the same trade again at the next support area. Sooner or later, he will be right. Often, however, the stock will trace out a new congestion pattern while it is testing the support area, as it did in figure 11-4. Thus, a position could be taken early as the stock completed a breakout at B_2.

IN A SIDEWAYS MARKET

The final possibility faced by the prospective purchaser is a market that is neither rising nor declining. It is, instead, in the midst of a broad sideways congestion area. The first and by now obvious tactic is to do nothing until there is some indication that the stock is about to begin a new aggressive rise. This would be signaled by the penetration of the upper limits of the congestion area, accompanied by high volume. Once this has been done, a position may be taken with a stop order below the lower limits of the area. Other traders with a strong fundamental opinion of the stock may make their purchases within the congestion area if the preceding trend is an uptrend. Since the odds are in favor of a continuation of the trend, the risk would be less than that which would prevail within an overall downtrend. In either case, a protective stop order is mandatory, since the battle has not been firmly resolved in either direction. If the breakout occurs on the downside, action must be delayed until the stock approaches the next support area below the market.

TIMING THE SHORT SALE

Once a trader has decided to sell short a fundamentally weak security, his problems of timing the commitment are approximately the same as the long trader. When he consults the chart, he will find that the stock is either in a process of rising, declining or moving sideways. If the reader were to reverse all of the tactics mentioned above for the timing of purchases, he would have the tactics of the short sale.

SUMMARY

The reader has just studied the beginnings of a system of trading which, if exploited to the fullest, could serve as a simple and effective trading approach. It would serve the trader who would like to continue to improve his fundamental analysis and yet add the most important aspects of technical analysis because of the improvements to trading they

140

offer. It is also a system that requires only a small overall change in the trader's speculative habits and requires little additional time.

This system allows the trader to immediately apply many of the charting principles as he learns them, without the usual lag in performance necessary when a new technique is introduced. Once this system has been used for a considerable period of time, the trader may then decide whether he would like to place future emphasis in his trading on the technical or on the fundamental approach. All the while, however, he should be not only becoming familiar with charts but should also be improving his fundamental analysis.

In the following chapters, this system will be gradually expanded to include more of the technical concepts discussed in the second section of this book in addition to a number of others. As the section progresses, the trading system will gradually become more technically oriented and aimed increasingly at the needs of the short-term trader. All through the section, however, the fundamental aspects of analysis will be given a place, leading in the end to a well-balanced system encompassing everything necessary for successful short-term trading.

Chapter 12
BLENDING FOR SUCCESS

The trading system described in the preceding chapter may be successfully utilized in several ways. Consider first the trader who has already had considerable experience and some success using fundamental analysis. The addition of chart analysis to his system can prove to be extremely helpful even while he continues to place the major emphasis of his analysis on the fundamentals. Without delving into the more refined charting techniques, he is able to continue his trading with a minimum of change in his approach, while taking advantage of the basic concepts of technical analysis. This simple and effective system, blending the technical with the fundamental approach, provides a well-rounded approach to trading. The trader wishing to continue to rely most heavily on fundamentals, although not enjoying the full advantages of technical analysis, may still improve his results dramatically.

This basic system may also, however, serve as an excellent training ground for the trader concentrating on developing his short-term trading skills to the fullest. If he is completely new to the stock market, he can use the system to develop his technical and fundamental skills jointly, while he is taking less risk than if he were to use either separately. If, on the other hand, he has already traded on fundamentals, he may learn the basics of technical analysis with a minimum of change and risk at the outset.

Whether the trader is satisfied to remain with the preceding system or goes on to develop more fully the technical system depends upon his objectives. The greater his interest lies in the very short price swings in the market, the more reliance he must be willing to place upon technical considerations. For it is axiomatic that the shorter the time period studied, the smaller is the influence upon stock prices of purely fundamental factors. In the very short run it is the technical approach that is the most helpful. Therefore, in this chapter will be developed a more refined system, one in which both techniques are again blended but one in which increasing emphasis will be placed upon technical analysis as the trader becomes more adept.

Unlike the simple trading approach of the previous chapter, the system developed here leaves much less to chance. It is a highly developed and organized framework for short-term trading. First, a definite list of trading stocks must be compiled and maintained. Once the list is compiled, primarily through fundamental analysis, increasing use is then made of the more refined charting patterns and techniques for timing. Finally, additional techniques for setting objectives are discussed. The result is a permanent system of trading that can be improved, refined and added to over the years and one that, if faithfully applied, will result in very satisfactory financial returns.

BUILDING THE TRADING LIST

The first step in building our complete trading system is essentially one of a fundamental nature. A list will be compiled of companies that demonstrate either present or potentially strong fundamental characteristics. All too often, the average trader wastes valuable time in the analysis of a security only to trade it once. After the trade, whether profitable or not, he usually abandons the stock to look for another. Isn't it more logical, since he is already familiar with the fundamentals of the firm, for the trader to continue his analysis in order to be ready for the next trading opportunity, particularly if there is good long-term growth potential in the stock? This is the reason for the maintenance of a definite trading list as an essential part of a successful trading scheme. Instead of searching anew for another candidate after each trade, the trader already has a list of sound stocks about which he is becoming increasingly knowledgeable. When sound technical analysis, for timing, is applied to this list of fundamentally sound securities, the result can only be one that is financially successful.

The selection of companies for the trading list, in keeping with the theme of this book, should combine the best of both fundamental and technical considerations. Until the trader becomes skilled in technical analysis, he should first stress thorough fundamental investigation of each firm before adding it to the list. Later, the analysis need not be quite so complete. Because this book is technical in scope, the details of the fundamental analysis are left to the reader. There are, however, a number of suggestions that can be made about the basic framework of the list and selection procedures.

INDUSTRY SELECTION

The best way to begin the selection of the list is a broad approach. Rather than immediately beginning the search for individual issues, the trader should first find those industries that are suitable to the trading list. Although fundamental analysis is being used at this stage, the trader must always keep the trading public in mind. Regardless of the quality of the fundamentals, it is the market following that a security or an industry enjoys which causes the wide price swings so necessary for short-term trading. It is industries such as electronics, computers, air pollution, medical technology, lasers and other futuristic industries that excite the speculating public. The trader would do well to ignore most of the mature industries to concentrate on those with exciting future possibilities. There are also other industries, mostly those that are cyclical in nature, that offer interesting trading possibilities at times. A glance at old long-term charts of the major stocks in the industry will uncover those that have enough price movement to qualify them for the trading list.

INDIVIDUAL SELECTIONS

Once the broad trading areas are defined, the trader can then give consideration to the individual stocks to add to his list. A good practice to follow is to select at least two—one of the leaders in each favored industry and one of the more speculative ones. There are reasons for this practice:

First of all, since there is a limit to the number of stocks that a trader can adequately follow, this enables him to cover as many industries as possible. Because there is a tendency for the companies of an industry to move together, an adequate number of different industries assures that trader of having a list of stocks which will be moving at all times.

Secondly, with this manner of selection, the trader will be

144

assured of having at least one higher-quality, relatively lower-risk stock to trade in each industry that he is interested in. He will also have at least one lower quality and usually low-priced stock to trade when the industry begins to move. Very often, although there is more risk taken, it is these low-quality stocks that generally have the widest price swings within the industry.

Finally, there is one more important reason for selecting stocks in this manner. Inevitably, it is the leader in the industry that begins to move first when the group is preparing an upward price swing. By watching the leader, the trader may often be given an early clue to buy the secondary stocks within the industry often right near their bottom. We will look at technical industry analysis at greater length in the next chapter.

BALANCED PRICES

Another important factor in the framework of the trading list is price balance. The list should not contain an overwhelming number of low-priced stocks nor should it be dominated by only high-priced glamour stocks or blue chips. For best trading results, the list should include stocks in every price range, with the majority of them in the $30 to $50 range—usually the best range for short-term trading. There are a number of reasons for this price diversification:

Most experienced traders have probably noticed that the stock market always tends to move in broad trends. For example, at times the blue chips or seasoned, matured stocks will tend to have the spotlight and, at other times, very low-priced and speculative stocks will dominate the trading. If the trader's list contains mostly low-priced stocks he will naturally be very happy and busy when they are surging. Because this particular phase in the market usually occupies only a small portion of an entire bull market, however, the trader would be very idle most of the time. It is true that he would always be enjoying the advantage of high leverage inherent in low-priced stocks, but he would also always be assuming a high degree of risk, because low-priced stocks are usually those of the poorest quality companies.

Nor is the trader any better off if his list is overpopulated by high-priced stocks. Certainly it is true that he will probably be dealing, for the most part, in much higher quality securities, but at the cost of being too cautious. He will in this case miss the opportunity of the wide price swings so often evident in the more unseasoned market favorites, as well as the leverage available from low-priced securities. In addition, many of the fledgling glamour industries are completely devoid of high-priced and well-established securities.

Once compiled, this list, diversified both by price and by industry, will serve as the trading base. The size of the list is limited only by the amount of time that the trader has available. The list should be constantly studied and, when the fundamentals turn sour, the stock should be dropped from the list. The trader should also be constantly on the alert for new industries or new firms to add to the list. Through this continuing study, the trader will be growing increasingly familiar with each stock and industry on the list.

Any trader with a reasonable amount of curiosity and time should have little trouble compiling a list far too large to be able to afford a position in each. He must then decide which to trade in at any given time. Here, of course, would be the failing of a purely fundamental system. It gives the trader little help in deciding which of these attractive stocks will move next. His only alternative is to take a position in as many stocks as possible and hope that they will soon start to move. (As any trader knows, it is always the stock you don't select that moves first. Then, as you liquidate the slow mover to follow the action, you find your original selection starts to move!)

In our complete trading system, however, our list of fundamentally attractive stocks is only the beginning. Added to sound fundamental analysis and constant vigilance will be a gradually improving technical approach to timing. Upon adding any security to the list, the trader will immediately begin to construct a chart on a daily basis and, if time permits, a weekly basis. These charts will solve the problem of being with the right stock at the right time.

TIMING THE TRADE

Once the trader is confident that he has a sound list of

146

trading stocks, he is ready to devote an increasing amount of his time to improving his timing through technical analysis. The experience gained in using the simple system of the previous chapter will serve as a foundation for chart analysis, but for effective short-term trading further refinements are needed. These will be supplied in this and the succeeding chapter.

As a first step in his advanced system of trading, the reader now begins to pay closer attention to the actual shapes of the congestion patterns studied earlier—of the familiar shapes that tend to recur consistently. Each of them offers a treasure of clues to future price trends if the chartist can read them properly. The system developed in this chapter will help him toward this end.

The trader now has a list of stocks fundamentally attractive for purchase, a chart of each with sufficient price history to identify trends, and an eagerness to begin his trading. The charts should be examined daily for evidences of the formation of any meaningful and familiar patterns. At first glance, the trader will see that the chart under study will show the stock in one of only several possible situations. Each situation must be handled differently.

THE DOWNTREND

If the stock, for example, is seen to be in a downtrend, and particularly when a well-defined downtrend line is evident, then regardless of how the fundamentals may appear the stock is not ready for a purchase. Assuming that the fundamental analysis was faultless, however, it is becoming a better buy with each decline. The chart should be studied closely for any early signs of a reversal pattern signaling the bottom. Many disillusioned traders will testify to the danger of guessing at the bottom of a stock with seemingly strong fundamentals rather than awaiting some technical sign of a true reversal. Needless to say, if one of the favored stocks is in a decided downtrend, the fundamentals should be checked closely once more for any possibilities of error. If the original analysis remains valid the stock may be an excellent trade once bottomed out. This will hopefully be signaled by one of the familiar reversal patterns studied in section two or, in the

147

case of a well-formed downtrend line, by a decisive breakout of the downtrend.

Suppose, for example, the stock under study, after a long decline, falls into a long sideways base pattern. The base pattern is singled out here because it is often a favorite place for commitment by many traders and also because it is probably the most mistraded of the reversal patterns. No other pattern tends to be more appealing after a long decline.

Since the stock has moved sideways for a considerable length of time it seems safe to assume that a bottom has been made. Often this is the case, especially when fundamental analysis shows it to be oversold and presumably a sound situation. If the trader is prepared for the possibility of having his trading funds tied up indefinitely, this is a safe price area to make a commitment, with a sell stop order immediately below the bottom of the base area. If, after a long sideways movement, the stock moves to a new low the position should be eliminated. If the trader was confident enough of the fundamentals at this low base price to buy without a stop order protecting his position, he should at a minimum check his fundamentals again if the base is broken.

The problem for the trader is that once the commitment is made, there is no assurance that the stock may not continue in its sideways pattern for weeks, months or even years. Probably more money is lost and trading time wasted on the base pattern than on any other pattern. This, no doubt, seems strange since it appears to be such a conservative place to make a commitment. Base patterns, however, are usually much longer than any other reversal pattern and may extend for long periods of time in spite of good fundamentals. The trader who commits his funds during one of these patterns often impatiently liquidates his position before the move begins. He ends up taking a small loss in addition to having his funds tied up for a considerable length of time.

The obvious solution is to do nothing when the pattern is discovered. The trader may merely make a note of the pattern and watch it closely for a breakout or, if the top of the pattern is clearly distinguishable, he may leave an open buy stop order slightly above the top of the pattern, and then take his position just as soon as the pattern is complete. In the meanwhile, he may use his trading funds more profitably elsewhere. It is possible that he may make several trades while he is waiting for the completion of the pattern. The open buy stop may be left in as long as the fundamentals do not deteriorate.

There are, of course, a number of other reversal patterns to alert the trader to a possible reversal, but they are not nearly so difficult to handle. They may be handled in several ways, depending upon the trader's assessment of the fundamentals. First, if the stock still appears to have extremely favorable fundamentals and it is in the midst of a reversal pattern, the trader may elect to take a position before the breakout with a close stop order at the appropriate price (see section II). If the fundamentals are not so clearly bullish, a position should be taken only upon the completion of the pattern. Finally, if the fundamentals are poor, the stock should be stricken from the trading list.

As a final warning, it must be remembered that triangles, rectangles, flags, pennants and other consolidation patterns are just as likely to appear within a downtrend as within an uptrend. They may serve merely as a resting phase before a new surge of selling. Don't mistake every congestion pattern for reversal.

THE UPTREND

The trader may also, of course, find his stock in a strong uptrend when he first studies its chart. This situation may be as difficult to trade as the downtrend, but at least the chart agrees with the fundamental analysis. If the uptrend has already carried the stock a great distance from the previous congestion area, the first notion of most traders is usually to give it up as "one that got away." Often, however, these are precisely the stocks that are the most likely candidates for immediate purchase. Since the most difficult job is to get the fundamentally attractive stock moving, most of the work has already been done.

The first step, in this situation, should be another check on the fundamentals of the stock. If the security is still under-priced or, at least, not drastically overpriced, there is no problem. The only question remaining is where to purchase

149

the stock. First, if the stock is in the process of forming a congestion area, caution should be exercised until the pattern has been completed. If the area is taking the shape of one of the familiar consolidation patterns of section II the trader may be given some indication of the outcome. If, for example, there is an ascending triangle forming and the fundamentals seem strong, a position may be taken prior to the breakout with a close protective sell stop below the pattern. Secondly, if the move has carried the stock only several points beyond the last congestion pattern, an immediate position may be taken with a protective stop below the previous congestion pattern. Finally, the situation that is the most dangerous is the stock that has been carried a considerable distance above any significant support area with only brief rests along the way. A powerful move of this type may be vulnerable to a drastic correction at any moment, or it may continue to elude the trader who cautiously awaits a sell-off. It is, unfortunately, precisely this type of move that most excites the short-term trader. The best practice in this case is to await the formation of a significant consolidation area where the position may be taken upon completion. If a trendline exists, a position may be taken on a pullback to the trendline if the fundamentals are sound. For the trader who is extremely enthusiastic about the fundamentals, the only other procedure would be to take the position and protect it as best as possible. A protective stop might be carried just below any previous minor top or bottom, and should be moved up behind any further advances.

Let us now examine the situation in which stock has already moved to the point where the trader feels that it has by far outpaced any fundamental value and is drastically overpriced. Very often, the most dynamic portion of the entire uptrend takes place after the stock has already reached the point where it is over-priced by any conservative standards. The momentum of the previous buying, along with the general excitement of speculation, pushes the stock through this final lunge, often aided by short-covering. It is always a safe bet to assume that the market will always overdo any move in either direction. How, then, can this be squared with our system of good fundamentals combined with astute technical analysis for timing? The only rule compatible with the system is as follows: If the position has already been taken before the move has carried to excess, it should be maintained until a valid technical signal is given that the trend is being reversed. If the excesses have occurred before a position can be taken, the stock is best forgotten unless there is a sizable correction. The trade is suitable only for those who are willing and able to place complete trust in technical analysis. This should be done only after the trader has used this present system for a considerable period of time with success.

Finally, it must be remembered that all good things usually come to an end. Each congestion pattern within the uptrend has the potential of reversing the move. If a stock, recently added to the favored list on the basis of its fundamental appeal, appears to be forming a top reversal pattern, then the technical and the fundamental are once more at odds. The procedure is the same as in the downtrend situation: The fundamentals should be rechecked for anything that might possibly lead to worsening sales or earnings (remember, the market is always looking ahead). Even though the original analysis still appears valid, no position should be taken until the suspected reversal pattern is resolved. If it turns out to be a false pattern, the completion of it might be just the right time for a position. The signal would be an upside penetration of some important resistance point, accompanied by high volume.

NO TREND

There is only one other situation in which the trader may find his stock when he consults the chart. Frequently, he will find no trend or pattern of any kind. There is, therefore, no clue as to the future direction or timing for any moves. Even here, the chart can be very helpful. In fact, the true test of charting skills is the ability to gain worthwhile information from the charts where there is seemingly none. It is situations like these that are usually the downfall of most beginning chartists. They expect to see textbook patterns staring back at them from any chart and begin to see them where they are not. This demonstrates again the value of a system that combines good fundamental analysis with beginning technical analysis—a combination which will keep the beginner from going broke before he develops the needed skills.

First of all, with a large and diversified list, the chances are very good that there will always be a few reasonably formed patterns for trades. If there are none, however, positions may still be taken by giving more weight to the fundamental considerations together with minor aids from the charts. For example, even in the most formless chart, there are always a number of minor tops or bottoms or small congestion areas which act as minor support or resistance areas. A long position may be taken when one of these test areas is penetrated on the upside with abnormal volume. In fact, if the fundamentals are extremely strong, any significant increase in volume might be a good signal of the beginning of a move. Any position taken may be immediately protected by a stop order below the closest support area.

The most important decision to be made by the trader is the amount of risk he is willing to take. Will he be willing to take a position simply upon the basis of good fundamentals or will he insist that both fundamental and technical considerations be favorable? The latter position is, of course, the most conservative, but he must be willing to sit idle until the right situation is available. Even if he is willing to take a position when the charts are neutral, as we have seen, the use of the chart is not entirely precluded. Minor support and resistance points may be used for stop orders or for objectives. Later, after the purchase is made, a pattern may eventually be formed that will confirm his decision or change his mind.

ADDITIONAL AID IN SETTING OBJECTIVES

Once a position is finally taken, the procedure is much the same as under the previous system. The position should be immediately protected with a stop order according to the simple system of the previous chapter and in accordance with the rules for stop orders with the individual patterns explained in section II. Once the protection is placed, it only remains to set a price objective for the trade. In this respect, a few refinements can be added to the theories of the previous chapter.

Each of the individual chart patterns examined in section II also have their own built-in objectives, once the breakout has occurred. Before looking at each pattern in turn, there is one general rule to keep in mind which applies to most patterns. That is, *the larger the pattern, the longer will be the move that follows the breakout.*

We had a brief exposure to this rule in the discussion of the "count." There it was stated that there exists a one-to-one relationship between the sideways expanse of the congestion area and the vertical move that follows the breakout and completion of the area. This same rule may be applied when discussing the individual patterns. The size may also be measured by the price range that the pattern encompasses, i.e., the height of the pattern. Many beginning chartists make the mistake of becoming overly excited over the price expectations of a stock simply because the shape of the pattern and the volume characteristics match the requirements. They pay no attention to the fact that the pattern may have developed in only a week and encompassed only a several point range. The long moves usually require extensive preparation, which is usually demonstrated by a long sideways movement as well as a wide price fluctuation. The only exceptions are the flag and pennant formations that will be discussed shortly. There are several other general rules to be discussed later. Now let us look at some of the individual patterns in figure 12-1.

HEAD AND SHOULDERS

The minimum price objective of the Head and Shoulders patterns is found by measuring the distance from the top of the head to the neckline. This distance is then projected downward from the breakout point to give the minimum expected move. As in all pattern objectives, all measurements are minimum expectations of the initial breakout. The move may eventually carry much further, particularly with such an important reversal pattern as the Head and Shoulders.

The objective for the Head and Shoulders bottom formation is measured in the same way and projected upward from the breakout area. Since the bottom formation is usually much shallower, the objective computed in this way is usu-

153

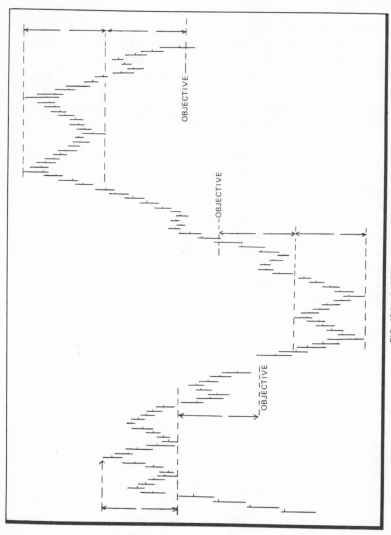

FIG. 12-1. PATTERN OBJECTIVES.

ally very conservative and the initial move from the breakout will carry much further. It is very interesting to note that with these seemingly very artificial devices, there will consistently appear at least a consolidation at about the objective.

DOUBLE TOP AND BOTTOM

Also in figure 12-1, it may be seen that the measurement of the price objective of the Double Top and Bottom formations are made in a similar manner. It is the height of the pattern that is measured and projected either upward or downward. It is measured from the fulcrum to the tops or bottoms. Like the Head and Shoulders, the objective is often only a short resting point, after which the move will resume.

TRIANGLES

The objectives of triangles and other consolidation patterns are somewhat different from those of the reversal patterns. An important difference is that triangle objectives may be counted upon to be much better indicators of the actual moves that follow the breakout. Very consistently, an important reversal or consolidation pattern will be formed at about the area of the triangle objective, while the objectives projected from the purely reversal patterns mentioned above are almost always surpassed by a considerable amount.

There are actually two different methods frequently used by chartists in setting objectives for triangle breakouts. The first is similar to that discussed with the reversal patterns. The height of each triangle is measured along the base of the pattern as shown in figure 12-2. It is measured along a line through the first contact point of the triangle and is the widest point of the formation. This distance is then projected from the breakout point and represents the minimum expected move.

The second and less exacting method is also shown in figure 12-2. Projection lines are drawn from the corners of the base of the triangle parallel to the side of the triangle opposite the breakout. In the case of the descending triangle, it is drawn from the lower corner of the base parallel to the downward slanting side. With the ascending triangle, it is an upward slanting line, parallel to the bottom side of the pat-

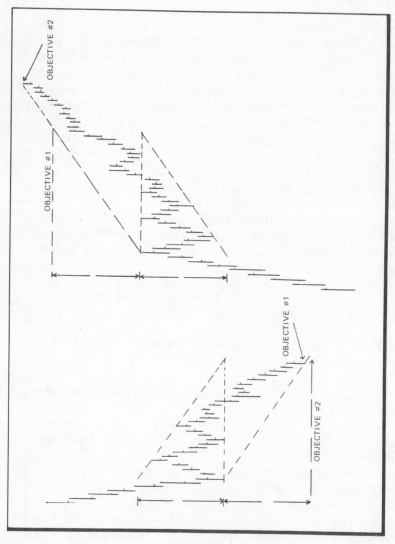

FIG. 12-2. TRIANGLE OBJECTIVES.

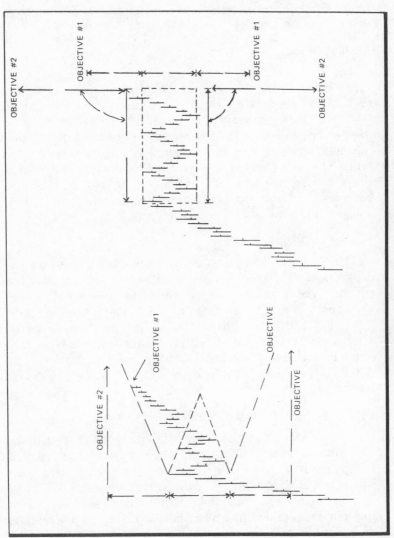

FIG. 12-3. TRIANGLE AND RECTANGLE OBJECTIVES.

tern beginning from the upper corner of the base.

Remember, in the symmetrical triangle the breakout may occur in either direction. Here, either of two lines may be drawn, depending upon the direction of the breakout. (See figure 12-3.) The objective of the breakout is met when prices reach this guideline.

RECTANGLES

The rectangle, like the symmetrical triangle, gives no advance signal of the direction of the breakout. The objectives, then, may be extended in either direction. They may also be set in two different ways. The height of the pattern may be used as one indication of the magnitude of the move. Often, however, the shape of the rectangle is one of narrow price range but an extended sideways movement. In these situations, a more accurate objective could be used to take into consideration the extended sideways consolidation. This analysis, previously discussed, is the count.

FLAGS AND PENNANTS

The Flag and Pennant patterns, as mentioned, are the exceptions to the general rule of objectives. The size of the patterns has no relation to the size of the move that follows the completion of the formation. They merely mark the half-way point within the move. That is, the move to be expected after the breakout will be of the same magnitude as that immediately preceding the formation of the pattern. The details of measurement were discussed fully in the chapter on high-velocity stocks.

OTHER GENERAL OBJECTIVES

In addition to the number of individual chart pattern objectives discussed above, there are several other general rules that have found popularity over the years. One such rule is called the "half-way" rule. This rule is extremely helpful to remember in situations in which there have been extensive price moves and in which there is no significant support or resistance area on the chart to aid the trader in deciding where to take his position. Assuming that he would like to take a position only after the move has corrected itself to

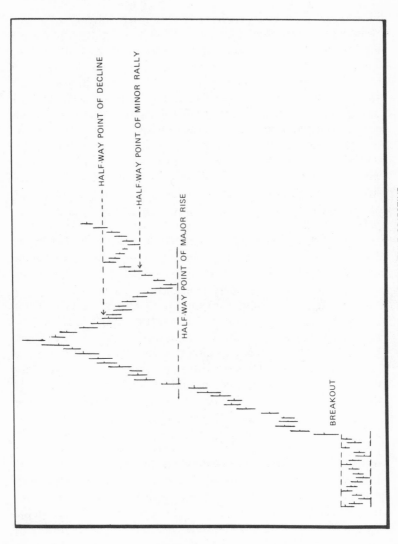

FIG. 12-4. HALF-WAY RULE OBJECTIVE.

some extent, it is difficult to decide just how big a correction is needed before the timing is right. A glance at figure 12-4 will demonstrate the principle.

According to the half-way rule, there is a general tendency for stocks to correct each price swing by roughly fifty per cent before resuming their trend. This may apply equally to long-term price movements as well as short trading swings. The stock in figure 12-4, for example, enjoyed an extensive move from the original breakout to its ultimate high without stopping to form any significant support areas. When the sell-off finally came, as the trader using this rule could have anticipated, the correction approximated half of the preceding rise. The trader could take his position here, expecting a test of the former high. The rally, as in figure 12-4, may again run into resistance at the half-way point of the decline from the high. The decline that follows may, in turn, retrace half of the rally from the original position, and so it goes. Each price movement may, in the absence of other patterns, retrace half of the preceding move. As long as each correction does not carry further than this fifty per cent, the original trend is still intact.

However, when the correction retraces more than fifty per cent of the preceding movement, a reversal of direction should be expected. In figure 12-4, if the sell-off of the major rise had carried even lower, the position should have been liquidated. The trader may also use this rule somewhat more conservatively by changing the percentage. A very bullishly moving stock, for example, should not suffer a correction of more than thirty to forty per cent. In practice, the trader will find that fast moving stocks will seldom see a correction of any move even approaching fifty per cent. Regardless of the percentage, however, this rule should be used only when no other helpful patterns are evident on the chart.

A final general rule to keep in mind is the fact that very often the consolidation patterns such as triangles and rectangles also tend to be found at the half-way point of major moves. That is, like the flags and pennants, a stock tends to move as far after the completion of one of these patterns as it traveled from the previous congestion pattern.

160

SUMMARY OF PRICE OBJECTIVES

At this point, the reader may be confused over the many types of objectives that have been discussed, hence a summary should be helpful. We began, in the previous chapter, with a simple system of setting objectives by the next support or resistance area. This basic system is, by far, the most effective. When combined with a system of sound fundamental analysis, it provides the foundation for a very effective trading system. When there are no significant areas or when they are too far apart to be helpful for short-term trading, the other refinements discussed are very helpful, and are necessary if the trader wishes to place increasing emphasis upon technical analysis. Whenever objectives formulated using the methods of this chapter are in conflict with a significant support or resistance area, the latter should naturally take precedence.

SUCCESS IS IN THE BLENDING

Throughout this book it has been maintained that the best approach to trading is the one that most successfully blends together the important ingredients of both the technical and the fundamental methods of analysis. By now, it is obvious that this is easier said than done. The most serious problem, that of organizing the two into a workable system, can be solved by the steps already mentioned in this book. Another serious problem is deciding, in each individual transaction, whether the fundamentals or the technical considerations should be the deciding factor. Most of the serious losses occurring in the market are those resulting from a refusal to believe what the market is saying. At times, it is best to ignore seemingly strong fundamentals when market action is very weak. At other times, the fundamentals may be strong enough to make it wise to ignore minor warning signals from the chart. A decision must be made for each transaction. The example below may serve to clarify a few approaches to proper blending.

Consider a situation in which the trader adds to his list a stock with outstanding fundamental attractiveness. He may, first of all, be willing to sacrifice some perfection in the

161

technical pattern to take a position, placing more trust in the fundamentals. Second, he may also be willing to take more chances in maintaining the position. He may, for example, be willing to ignore minor chart signals like a penetrated trendline or small patterns, and be driven to admit his error only in the case of a perfectly formed and potentially powerful reversal formation.

Contrast this example with a situation in which the stock added to the list has only above average fundamentals. Here, the trader should be much less willing to take a chance on the technical pattern. He should take a position only when very strong technical signals are given, and once the position is taken, he should be much less willing to argue with the market. He will be quick to liquidate his position at the first minor sell signal. Here it is important to remember the basis upon which the position was taken. Too often, a trader takes a position on technical considerations and when things go wrong, he deludes himself into building a stronger fundamental case for the stock rather than to take his technical medicine.

A final example is the situation in which a position was taken in a stock with strong fundamentals and which subsequently enjoyed a sizable rise. Once the stock has appreciated to the extent that all of the favorable fundamentals have been overdiscounted, fundamental analysis should give way completely to technical analysis, and technical signals of a possible top should be the prime consideration.

The final aid to successful blending is experience. In this book, we have stressed a gradually progressive reliance upon technical analysis, never abandoning completely the fundamentals. As the reader becomes more experienced with charting techniques, he may gradually place more reliance on charts in his decisions. As also mentioned, he may stop anywhere along the way. That is, he may stop with the simple system of the previous chapter and continue to place almost full reliance upon the fundamentals. Or, he may continue to the more advanced system outlined in this chapter, particularly if he is more interested in short-term trading. Finally, as he has greater confidence in his charting prowess, he may add one final step in his charting/fundamental system:

While maintaining the present system utilizing the well-studied list of fundamentally secure stocks, the trader may also decide to take an occasional position almost solely upon technical considerations. This step should, of course, be taken only by those who have already used charts extensively with a reasonable amount of success. Even here, the fundamentals need not be completely abandoned but may again be blended. Fundamental analysis, perhaps less extensive than that performed on those stocks in the list, may be used to weed out those trades that offer an unreasonably high degree of risk.

To take this additional step in his trading system, it should be necessary for the trader to have access to a charting service. The charts that he is maintaining on the stocks in his trading list should be enough to occupy most of his time. The charting service will enable him to watch a much larger list of stocks simply for interesting technical patterns. By watching these stocks and applying a quick fundamental analysis to each, he will find that all candidates will fall into one of four categories:

1. Doubtful chart pattern . . . . Poor fundamentals
2. Excellent chart pattern . . . . . Good fundamentals
3. Doubtful chart pattern . . . . . Good fundamentals
4. Excellent chart pattern . . . . Poor fundamentals

Once again, safety can be brought into each decision by combining both techniques. Certainly #1 should be eliminated from any consideration. The second combination is obviously the most risk-free trade. The trader who insists upon only this combination is undoubtedly headed for greater success. The final two combinations, although less conservative, may also offer good trades to the more venturesome. Here, however, the trader is left again with the problem of deciding to which of the two approaches to lend the most weight. In any case, under a system that blends both techniques, the trader is free to decide just how much risk he is willing to assume in his trading. The patient trader who insists upon the best of each (#2) certainly assumes very little risk.

Whether the trader takes the final step of increasing reliance upon technical analysis or remains with the original trading list of well-researched stocks, the critical point of the trade is the initial positioning of the stock. If this is done right, the only remaining problem is the decision of how much profit to accept. This focuses attention upon the breakout, which is probably the most important aspect of technical analysis. In the following chapter, the final touches will be given to the reader's technical education by looking at the breakout in detail.

Chapter 13

THE BREAKOUT

Much has already been said about the breakout. It signals the completion of a significant consolidation or reversal congestion area on the chart. It also signals the beginning of a significant price movement and sizable profits for the trader who can successfully interpret the chart. An incorrect interpretation here will, of course, lead to immediate losses. To the trader who confines his commitments to an improved list of fundamentally sound securities, the error might not be quite so serious. But to the trader who has taken the advanced step of making commitments solely upon technical considerations, with only minor fundamental analysis, the consequences may be much more damaging. Since he is more interested in short-term trading, which makes an increasing reliance upon charts a necessity, his commitments will be more strongly influenced by the breakout than by the underlying fundamentals. His analysis of the breakout, then, is crucial.

We have already seen that every breakout is not necessarily a valid one that faithfully follows through for at least the minimum objectives. The pattern may also be misinterpreted by the chartist. For the trader who makes the right decision at the breakout, it only remains for him to decide how much profit to try for. If he is wrong here, his only decision is where to cut his losses. Skill in avoiding the losing situations can only come through long practice with charts and perhaps many expensive lessons. There are, however, a number of ways to limit the risk of bad commitments. It is the purpose of this chapter to look at the breakout under as many different situations as possible, in an effort to show the trader how to avoid many of the more obvious pitfalls and riskier trades.

The first important lesson that must be learned by the beginning chartist is that in technical analysis, as in most disciplines, there is a wide gulf between theory and practice. Most beginning chartists are guilty of becoming overly mechanical in their analysis of breakouts, and immediately take positions on a breakout that may only vaguely resemble one of the patterns they have learned. When disappointments follow, they blame the system. They are guilty of treating charting as a science rather than the art that it is. Like any theory, it cannot be put into practice under perfectly controlled circumstances. There is plenty of room for good qualitative thinking and plain common sense, for each potential breakout situation is unique and must be studied closely. While in one the odds of success are greatly stacked in favor of the trader, others may involve a great deal of risk. It is only practice on the battleline that will teach the trader how to distinguish one from the other. Although the skilled chartist who knows how to cut his losses short and use stop orders properly can take positions in many of the riskier situations, the average trader would do well to avoid them in favor of the more conservative trades.

The best approach, then, is to eliminate as many of those breakouts as possible that might turn out to be false. This calls for patience on the part of the new chartist, which is often what he has the least of. He must be ready to leave a part of his trading funds idle at times while he is waiting for the ideal breakout. His patience will be rewarded, however, with a much lower number of failures. In the pages that follow, a number of refinements to breakout analysis will be listed, all aimed at eliminating the potential false breakout. In keeping with the theme of this book, the refinements are not only of a technical nature but also of a fundamental nature.

TECHNICAL CONSIDERATIONS

CHECK YOUR PATTERN

The first step in the breakout checklist should be an examination of the pattern itself. Remember, the closer the pattern resembles the theoretical textbook pattern, the more likely the chances of success. For example, if the suspected pattern is a Head and Shoulders, is it symmetrical and are there well-defined tops or bottoms? Is there a well-defined support area at the neckline? Is it a broad pattern formed after a substantial price movement? Whatever the suspected pattern, questions of this nature should be asked to determine how closely the pattern fits all of the requirements. Every deviation from the perfect pattern is an added element of risk.

Remember also that the size of the pattern is crucially important, in that it is one of the best indications of the extent of the possible move. A well-formed pattern might be rejected if the potential move is not large enough to warrant the risk of the commitment, since it generally takes a large pattern to reverse a substantial price movement.

However, it is in the analysis of the pattern itself that the beginner commits most of his errors, since he is prone to see patterns where none exist and to accept too many that should be rejected. If he learns to be more discerning from the beginning, he will avoid many expensive lessons later.

VOLUME

While the chartist is examining the shape of the pattern in detail, he should not neglect the volume characteristics inherent in each pattern. Formations that exhibit volume characteristics close to those expected in the perfect pattern have a greater chance of success. Continuing the example of the Head and Shoulders top, is the volume high on the left shoulder and head while diminishing greatly during the formation of the right shoulder? If not, some doubt should be cast on the potential success of the breakout.

If the pattern is a consolidation formation such as a triangle or rectangle, the volume should be substantially reduced during the formation of the pattern. If an upside breakout is under study, an accompanying burst of trading is absolutely necessary.

Remember also the general theory of volume. All things being equal, a bullish price movement is one that exhibits expanding volume on rallies and declining trading on all sell-offs and consolidation areas. The stock that has been exhibiting these characteristics before the formation of the pattern in question has one more bullish point in its favor.

After the trader has completed the first two steps of this qualifying checklist he may already have an outstanding trade possibility. If both the shape and the volume characteristics of the pattern resemble closely the textbook examples of the pattern in question much of the risk has been removed. The checklist need not end here, however, for there are still a number of other ways to take the risk out of the trade.

GAPS AND PULL-BACKS

The pull-back that so often occurs following a breakout is another important indicator of the success of the breakout. The conservative chartist may wait for a pull-back following a breakout before taking his position. Although he knows that all breakouts do not include a pull-back, he is willing to take the chance of missing a trade rather than to ignore the valuable clues to be gained from observing the pull-back first. An analysis of the volume characteristics of the breakout and pull-back may either cast doubt on the validity of the breakout or give it a further vote of confidence. Consider first the upside breakout:

The upside breakout must, as we know, be accompanied by a sizable increase in trading. Once the initial drive of the breakout is spent and the pull-back begins, the volume should decline precipitously. If the breakout is to be successful, the price of the stock should work slowly back to the pattern in dull trading. Once the pull-back is completed, usually well above the breakout point, the stock will then begin to rally again, accompanied by another sharp increase in trading. In fact, the volume following the completion of the pull-back is often much higher than that accompanying the breakout. The breakout that enjoys a pull-back afterward that conforms to these requirements has one more plus factor toward its validity. If, on the other hand, the volume on the pull-back were higher than that on the breakout, the entire pattern may be held in suspect.

The analysis of the pull-back that follows a downside breakout is quite similar. Starting with the breakout, it may be recalled that the downside breakout does not require an increase in volume to be valid. The volume accompanying the pull-back, however, is potentially significant. When the stock begins to pull back up to the pattern following a breakout, the rally should be a rather dull affair, with little increase in trading. High volume on this rally is a good indication that a false breakout occurred. Quite often, the volume that was missing when the breakout occurred comes into the market once the pull-back is completed and the stock has begun to decline once again.

A further qualification may be added to the breakout by considering the presence of a gap accompanying either the upside or the downside breakout. The reader learned in section II that the appearance of a gap during the breakout is a good indication of the force behind the breakout move and consequently a further plus mark toward its validity. If the checklist has been followed up to this point and the trader is still looking for a further reason to make his commitment, the appearance of a gap can give him additional courage. It is one more safety item that the conservative trader may insist upon before accepting the technical verdict. The trader, depending upon the amount of risk he wishes to assume, may insist upon as many of those mentioned thus far before making his decision.

CHART HISTORY

It may be obvious by now that there is no end to the qualifications that may be made of each breakout and potential trade. Obviously, the more qualifications that are demanded of the breakout, the fewer will be the trades available. Just as certain is the fact that the ones that are accepted will enjoy greater odds for success. Trading may be as safe as the trader is willing to make it. The more patient he is and the more willing to take the time for careful and intelligent study of each trade, the more successful he should be.

At the same time that the trader is examining the chart for the safety factors so far mentioned he should also be performing another important operation. Before taking any position, the trader should examine past charts of the stocks to determine its past history. It is interesting to note that many stocks exhibit well-defined long-term trading characteristics. For example, a particular stock may show a history of always forming triangles when consolidating and Head and Shoulders patterns whenever reversing its trend. At the same time, another stock may have a history of false breakouts, particularly when breaking out of a pattern. Certainly, if this were true of the stock in question, extra caution should be applied

169

and more buy indicators demanded.

The more recent price history of the stock may also give valuable information regarding the potential success of the breakout. The stock that has enjoyed an extensive move without a rest is obviously more vulnerable to a large correction than one that has paused often to rest. A false breakout from a suspected consolidation pattern within such a move would be very costly. Remembering that most consolidation patterns may also be reversal patterns on occasion, the trader should exercise greater caution in following the breakout from a consolidation pattern in these circumstances. It can be seen, then, that the trader may be more daring or more conservative depending upon the situation. That is, he may insist on more or less of the qualifying safety devices mentioned up to this point. A study of the past history of the stock will often give him the key to his approach. The longer that a chartist works with charts, the more he will be able to learn from a quick study of the past price history of the stock.

GROUP ANALYSIS

There is also a further helpful aid to separating the potential malfunctioning chart breakout from the valid ones. This aid, unlike the others, concentrates not on the individual stock in question but on the industry of which it is a part. A quick study of the charts of other stocks in the same industry will often give the chartist valuable information regarding the future success of the suspected breakout. While this is especially true of those industries which tend to move as a group, it is also true to varying degrees of all other industries. Not only do the stocks of the companies tend to move together, but they also tend to form similar patterns on their charts at the same time. The wise chartist, as a further check before committing his funds, should first look at as many charts of similar stocks as possible.

Although the stocks in a group tend to move roughly together, there are always those that tend to lag and others that tend to lead the group. The benefits of this analysis should now be obvious. If a number of the leaders in the industry have already formed very similar patterns to the one in question and have broken out on the upside, for example, then a similar breakout from our pattern is probable. If, on the

170

other hand, the stock under study enjoyed an upside break-out while a quick check shows many downside breakouts in the industry, the trader should be suspicious, regardless of how favorable many other signs may be.

Even when clearly discernible patterns are not available in the other stocks, this method of analysis can still be very helpful. The experienced chartist will soon develop a good eye for spotting the general condition of the industry from a set of charts. Very often, a set of industry charts will look somewhat bearish in tone, without well-defined patterns. Certainly an upside breakout of one of the stocks in an overall bearish industry should be suspected.

There is another group phenomena that is also very interesting and profitable to know. There is a pronounced tendency for the leaders or high-quality companies of an industry to lead and for the speculative or secondary companies to lag in any major price movement. The move in the secondary stocks at times may lag behind the leaders by many months. The chart is very helpful in signaling the beginning of the secondary movement to those traders that missed the start of the industry move. It is usually these speculative stocks that offer the greatest profit potential to the trader. Best of all, the trader has advance notice of their move. There is also a very good explanation for this phenomenon: Institutional investors such as the large mutual funds, banks, insurance companies and other professional investors that maintain well-trained research staffs are most often the first to discover the changing trends of an industry. These institutions, by preference and often by law, buy only the more seasoned leaders within the industry. Later, when the public finally becomes aware of the potential of the industry, they will begin to purchase, as a rule, the secondary stocks of the industry, accounting for the delayed move. Regardless of the reasons for this very consistent lag, it is one of the most profitable bits of knowledge a trader can know.

FUNDAMENTAL CONSIDERATIONS

SECURITY ANALYSIS

The trading system developed up to this point has, of course, already been well spiced with security analysis. If the

171

trader has maintained a trading list of fundamentally sound securities it is naturally presumed that he has already performed an exhaustive security analysis upon the stock before he has added it to the list. It is also presumed that he has continued to update his fundamental information and has become even better acquainted with the stock. The breakout, then, has already been qualified further by the fundamentals.

If the trader has, however, reached the point where he is beginning to select his trades solely from attractive chart patterns rather than from his list, then this further qualification should be insisted upon. Before taking his commitment, the trader should, at least, perform enough fundamental analysis to eliminate the obviously poor fundamental risk.

NEWS ANNOUNCEMENTS

A perhaps less obvious fundamental consideration to be made in testing a breakout is the effect of current news announcements upon the future success of the breakout. The reaction of the stock market to news announcements is, without a doubt, the most confusing market event to most beginning investors or traders. The confusion is abetted by the myriad market slogans on the subject such as: "buy on bad news," "sell on good news," "buy on the rumor—sell on the news," and finally, "buy on strike news—sell on the settlement." It is small wonder that such confusion exists. Yet the short-term trader who does not utilize some form of technical analysis is forced to trade, for the most part, on these news announcements.

Much of the confusion may be cleared up immediately when the trader ultimately learns that business news is almost always "discounted" to some extent. We learned earlier that insiders and their friends and relatives together with a much smaller number of shrewd analysts usually know of the news before it is announced publicly. Being of sound mind all, they have also already acted upon the news by buying or selling their stock. When the public announcement is finally made, they are already taking their profits, along with others who might have made commitments based upon the rumors of the news. This action will usually cause the stock price to move in a direction opposite to that expected from the

172

announcement. If the news was bullish, for example, the selling for profits would ordinarily cause the stock to sell off on the news. Knowing all of this, however, does not necessarily mean that the trader is now ready to trade the news successfully. He still has the problem of getting the news fast enough to take advantage of it, and he must also be able to assess the potential reaction to the news and how much of it has already been discounted.

Strict charting, of course, tells the chartist to ignore completely all business news along with all fundamentals because it is all reflected in the chart. This point is demonstrated again and again to anyone who works with charts for a reasonable length of time. The action of the insiders will quite often be very obvious on the chart of the stock long before the news announcement is made. Their very act of discounting the news is enough, in these cases, to give the chart a favorable supply-demand relationship, resulting in a breakout long before the publicity of the news. How, then, does this relationship fit into the system of trading here being developed?

Since methods of qualifying each breakout before taking a position are being discussed, news announcements are an important addition to the list of qualifications. Although it is very difficult to state clearly the possible relationship between business news and each individual breakout, there is one handy general rule to remember: *the breakout that occurs totally in the absence of any news is to be preferred.*

The breakout that occurs without any outside help such as a news announcement is naturally stronger than the one that requires help. It demonstrates that the technical condition of the stock is strong. The news announcement should only be grounds for caution, however, and not for immediate rejection of the breakout. First of all, the news might have been only partially discounted and only coincidentally occurred with the breakout. Secondly, there are a number of other situations where the position should be taken anyway. These will be discussed later.

On the other hand, there is the stock that built a bullish pattern partly as a result of the discounting buying. Without the potential news announcements, it would not have had the technical strength to complete such a pattern. The news announcement, however, brings in enough new buyers to finally force a breakout. It is here the chartist may blunder, by taking a position just as the breakout occurs. The news might have been just good enough to cause the breakout and the chartist is left holding the stock at the highest price of the entire move.

Since a news announcement may either help along a breakout or completely negate it, it is obvious that it should be one of the more important factors in our list of breakout qualifications. Although the breakout that accompanies a news announcement need not be immediately abandoned, a great deal of caution should be used until the news is analyzed. If the chartist has already checked-off a number of the qualifications on the list and has found the breakout to be valid, he may ignore the occurrence of the news announcement. If his analysis up to this point shows the breakout to be on shaky ground, he should either abandon the breakout or, at least, examine very carefully the nature of the news announcement. How, then, can the nature of the news be analyzed? What should he look for?

When examining the news, the trader should attempt to place the news into one of two general categories, depending upon the duration of the effect of the news upon the stock price. If the news is such that, once announced, no further benefit may accrue to the company, it is a negative factor for the potential success of the breakout. If, on the other hand, the news portends further favorable news and benefits accruing to the company, it should be counted upon as another plus qualification, and if all other checkpoints are favorable a position should be taken.

One example of the negative type of announcement to the chartist is the stock-split. Almost invariably, the rally that occurs with the announcement of a stock-split marks the short-term high for the stock. If the stock has enjoyed a sharp rally preceding the announcement, the stock may be expected to begin to sell off the same day as the announcement. It is news announcements like the stock-split, the moderate increase in earnings or dividends, the change in management, new stock offerings, secondary offerings, and other announcements of less far-reaching effects upon the stock that cause the chartist trouble. If any of these announcements occur following a substantial unexplained rally, a sell-off will almost certainly follow.

The earnings report, under some circumstances, may also serve as an example of the positive type of new announcement. If, in addition to reporting good earnings, the company also gives glowing estimates for the year ahead, the report may have more lasting effects upon the price of the stock. An announcement of a merger may fall into either category. If the merger appears to be certain with definite terms given, it probably marks the end of the rally. If, however, the terms are vague and speculators are kept guessing, quite often the breakout may be only the beginning of the move and, if all other indicators are favorable, a position should be taken.

As the reader may realize by now, it is impossible to classify all news announcements neatly into several categories of good, bad or indifferent. A fine and practiced eye is needed to sift out the important from the unimportant, the exciting from the mundane, the news that will sustain a breakout from the news that will end the move. Nor is there any direct relationship between the nature of the news and the rally that occurs before it is announced. Very frequently, the moderate insider buying that occurs in response to a pending minor news announcement is fanned into a bigger move than is warranted as rumors and unfounded stories make the rounds of the brokerage houses. Often, what is a relatively unimportant news announcement, like a small dividend increase, is transformed, via the rumor route, into the most unlikely of stories of mergers, ets. It is small wonder that the actual announcement of seemingly good news is met not only by profit-taking by insiders but also by the disappointed selling of many who had expected much more.

There is one further key to analysis of the news that should always be kept in mind. This key, in a word, is "mystery." Mystery is the one ingredient that is always necessary to maintain a price move. When all of the bullish news is out, and all of the future implications of the news as far as its effects upon earnings can be readily seen by all, the news is of no further interest to the speculator. For the short-term

175

trader, this is often the best time to eliminate the position. By the same token, when all of the bad news regarding a company is known by all and fully discounted, it is often the time for a rally just when things look the blackest. A few examples may be helpful.

An excellent example of this theory is the company that announces the discovery of a major oil or mineral find. If an accurate estimate of the value of the find is given, together with its exact effect upon earnings growth for the next several years, the market will discount all of the effects of the discovery if it has not already done so, and the move will be over. If, on the other hand, few financial details are given at the time of the announcement, the imaginations of the speculators will soon go to work. Brokerage firms and investment advisory services begin to make guesses as to future effects upon earnings and as to the total value of the find. Rumors become rampant. Each earnings estimate and each rumor adds fuel to the fire, and the news announcement, instead of ending the move, only marks the beginning. The stock-wise corporate executive, interested in high prices for his stock, has learned not to spill all the news at once. As favorable details are gradually given out by the company, earnings estimates revised by brokerage firms and services, and rumors circulated, the stock continues to climb, and often the move takes the stock to a price much higher than originally warranted by the news. The same reasoning applies also to announcements of technological or scientific breakthroughs, new products, mergers, and many other types of news. Remember, the key word "mystery."

GENERAL CONSIDERATIONS

Up to this point, we have been considering means for eliminating the risks of false breakouts on an individual stock basis. It is also helpful to study other influences upon individual chart patterns that are more general in nature. The first to come to mind should be the stock market as a whole.

TRADE WITH THE TREND

Needless to say, the potential success of a breakout can be substantially influenced by the condition of the entire market. Taking a position in a stock that has just completed an upside breakout is naturally more risky in a declining market than in a rising one. The trader who is short in a bull market obviously suffers the same disadvantage.

There are, of course, always a number of stocks that will be able to move against the trend. The odds, however, are very decidedly against the chartist, and even more so the fundamental trader, who tries to pick those few among the many that will fight the trend. Many experienced chartists, however, claim that charts are even more helpful in a declining market than in one that is rising. Their reasoning is that because fewer stocks are rising and because most chart patterns are uninspiring, the bullish breakout stands out and is difficult to overlook. The stock will tend to stand out even more on the ticker tape. There is certainly much truth in these statements. There is a hard core of traders who must always be busy trading even if it means giving back all the profits they made in the preceding bull market. Their tendency, like the trading public as a whole, is to be on the long side. Because the choice of rising stocks is so limited, these traders tend to pile on a few stocks, often causing rises that carry much further than they might if the overall market were bullish. Consequently, when the trader is right he may have a very successful trade. When he is wrong, however, he is very, very wrong, and the odds favor his being wrong.

The beginning chartist, expecting miracles from his charts, too often attempts to fight the trend. For most, it would be much better to save these dangerous trades until he has become much more skillful with the use of charts and stop-loss orders. Until then, he would be far better off to treat the condition of the market as merely one more plus or minus check among the qualifications already mentioned for the breakout. If he has found, for example, a downside breakout with all other qualifications also pointing down, he may then look to the condition of the market as a determining factor. If he feels stocks are in a general bear market or, at least, a short-term decline, it would be a plus factor in his analysis, giving him one more good reason for taking a short position.

Most traders, however, are more likely to be long-oriented and looking only for stocks to purchase. Under these circumstances, the market mentioned above would be a minus factor in the list of qualifications. If all the other qualifications point to a rally, and if the trader decides to fight the trend, he should at least check everything once more before taking a position. Although short-selling is inherently more dangerous than trading from the long side, in the case of the broadly declining market the trader would be far better off to search out the patterns where the majority of qualifications point to a valid downside breakout. If he refuses to trade from the short-side he would be advised to stay on the sidelines until he has either a bullish market trend or at least one that is neutral in tone.

In general, the best method for the beginning chartist is to trade only from the long side in what appears to be a bullish market. It is here where charts seem to be the most helpful. Even in the strongest market rise, all stocks do not take their major moves at once. The bull market is, instead, a series of rotating groups and individual stocks. It is in the general bull market that the highest number of upside breakouts tend to be valid ones. In the bear market, although some stocks are rising, all too often what looks like a perfect upside breakout turns out to be a false one, leaving the trader on the wrong side of the market. All of the borderline breakouts, many of which stand a good chance of success in a bull market, are not strong enough to fight the declining trend of the entire market.

If the trader has had considerable experience and feels he is ready to fight the trend, he should follow a few simple rules. First, he should take no shortcuts on the list of qualifications. He should insist that each breakout satisfies all qualifications. Secondly, he should not fail to use a protective stop order immediately upon taking a position. He should add a further qualification to the list: A position will not be taken unless the chart demonstrates a well-defined place for a close stop-order. When taking a long position in a declining market he should also insist upon extremely strong fundamentals, while short positions should be taken in a bull market only if there is a strong possibility of continuing weak fundamentals.

The influence of news announcements upon chart break-outs has already been discussed in detail. The corporate earnings report is no exception, and the chart breakout that occurs just before or in conjunction with an earnings report should put the chartist on his guard. Because the earnings reports are such common news announcements it would be well to consider them separately. Since most companies report their earnings on a calendar-year basis, there are four periods of time during each year when the chartist should be especially alert. The first three weeks following the end of each quarter in March, June, September, and December are critical, as it is during these times that rumors are flying and insiders buying in anticipation of the flood of earnings reports that are soon to be announced. It is also during these times that many favorable patterns may be breaking out to lure the chartist into taking a position, only to see a sell-off when the earnings report is announced. If the chartist can anticipate that the report will be forthcoming, he would be much safer to wait until the report is made and then observe the action of the chart. It is often very easy to pinpoint the exact day of the announcement, since the earnings results are often announced at the corporate dividend meetings that are usually held at roughly the same times. The dates of the coming dividend meetings are publicized well in advance. If the breakout is occurring just before the known dividend meeting, the chartist can count on at least a pull-back to the pattern when the earning are made public.

Another cause for concern to the chartist during these periods is the direction of the market as a whole, since it is one more source of danger to the breakout that occurs during these periods. It is very common for the market to suffer a broad setback just after the flood of public earnings announcements is made. This is quite normal, since there is somewhat of a void following each period. All of the news is out, insiders have discounted the news and then have taken profits, while fundamental traders, encouraged by the favorable earnings reports, have taken positions on the news, only to suffer an immediate loss. Everyone is waiting to see what is going to happen next. Although this type of lethargic sell-off may not be strong enough to turn back the truly strong breakout, many weaker breakouts will not have the strength to move up through the short-term decline.

The trader has two good reasons, then, for being cautious during the four periods of the year when earnings reports are due. Any positions that he takes during these periods should satisfy as many of the qualifications as possible. Close stop orders should also be used, to protect each position against not only the sell-offs that may occur when the favorable news finally breaks, but also against the surprise earnings report that may be unfavorable. In any case, it would probably be best to refrain from initiating new positions if the earnings report is near.

TAX-LOSS SELLING SEASON

Another perilous time of the year for chartists is the season of tax-loss selling. Although the weight of tax selling and switching is felt throughout November and December, it is particularly the last several weeks in December and the first several in January that are the most dangerous. The danger lies in the fact that there are forces at work during this period that tend to unduly influence and distort the technical picture of many stocks, and will cause breakouts where there should be none. They will trap the unwary chartist into taking positions where he is doomed to failure from the outset. Hence, we have an addition to our list of qualifications for valid breakouts.

Consider first the last few weeks of December when tax-selling is at its height. It is during this eleventh hour liquidation that many stocks are depressed severely and, more important, *temporarily*. This heavy liquidation leads to many downside breakouts from patterns or through important support areas. A stock, for example, that may be in the process of forming an important bottom pattern may be suddenly interrupted by this wave of selling. On a strict technical basis, the stock may appear to be an excellent short sale candidate or at least for a long liquidation when, in fact, after the abnormal selling subsides it may resume its bottom reversal pattern. The inability of the chartist to recognize this abnormal selling spree for what it is will draw him into many false breakouts. Special attention should be given to any breakout during this period, but particularly to those downside breakouts in the stocks that are most obviously bearing the brunt of the tax-selling. They are the stocks that are near their low of the year, making new lows or far below their highs of the year. They are the stocks that are sold the hardest in the closing days of the year and hence most likely to be experiencing downside breakouts. Significantly, they are also the stocks that will rally the strongest in the first weeks of the new year.

It is not, however, only the weak stocks that the chartist must be wary of during this period. Some upside breakouts may be equally as dangerous. Just as the stocks that have done poorly during the year are absorbing their worst selling in this period, the best performance stocks of the year often have their best rallies during this same period. It is a case of the rich getting richer and the poor getting poorer. Those that are taking their losses for the year are switching into those stocks that they wished they had purchased during the year. Almost every year this pattern is reversed in the first weeks of the new year. That is, the worst stocks of the old year are the strongest in the first few weeks of the new year as selling pressure is removed and the stocks rally from their oversold positions. At the same time, the glamour stocks of the old year sell off heavily from delayed profit-taking by those who want to register their profits in the new year and thus have a full extra year before paying taxes. Imagine the chagrin of the tax-switcher who sees the stock he sold rally strongly, while the one he purchased drops precipitously. It should also make the beginning chartist wonder as to the efficacy of his charts.

Obviously, any short position taken as downside breakouts are occurring in the tax-loss candidates will be in trouble for at least a few weeks in January. Those following the upside breakouts of the glamour stocks of the old year will be in the same hot water. Although the problem may be temporary in nature, there is the question of whether good short-term trading procedure would allow the trader to suffer such a sizable paper loss, assuming that the principle of cutting losses short is followed. Naturally, there are many breakouts during this period that will turn out to be valid and the chartist need not abstain completely. The incidence of tax-selling, however, is certainly an important qualification in the analysis of any breakout during this crucial time of the year. Indeed, it can be so important that the chartist should follow only those breakouts that he is especially confident of.

There is, finally, a positive side to the tax-selling season. If one would like to abandon the charts temporarily, he may find a pleasantly consistent trading scheme that may return him ten to twenty per cent profit in several weeks. It is probably obvious by now that a diversified position in the hardest-hit stocks of the last days of the year might be a dynamic portfolio for the first few weeks of the new year. This is precisely the trading scheme that has been successful for many traders. The trader who is buying those stocks that are being sold the hardest at the end of the year has been rewarded very consistently in January. This is often accomplished by going entirely against the chart theory as explained here, and may sound strange in this technically oriented book. But it is a good way to emphasize the powerful force working against the chartist at this time of the year. Those stocks exhibiting what appears to be valid technical sell signals are the same stocks that will very shortly lead the market upward in January, the most consistent upward month in the year.

SHORT INTEREST

A final factor to consider before taking a position in a suspected breakout is the short interest position of the stock. From an earlier chapter, the reader should be acquainted with the concept of short interest and the short sale. The general rule to follow is that the higher is the short interest in any security, the better the prospects for a bullish move.

Because each short sale must eventually be "covered" by buying an equivalent number of shares, each short sale represents a potential buy order. Naturally, the more shares that have been sold short and not yet covered, the greater is this reservoir of purchasing power. Also, because the average short position is maintained for a much shorter duration than the average long position, this buying power is a very important consideration for the *short* term.

To assess the potential effect upon the security in question, it is necessary to compare the short position with the number of shares outstanding and with the "floating supply." The floating supply concept considers that some stock, although outstanding, can not be expected to become a part of the trading volume. This stock may be held for control purposes by management, by institutional investors, by founding families, etc. When this stock is subtracted from the total shares outstanding and compared to the short position, the true potential effects of the possible short-covering on the price of the stock may be discovered.

When applying this concept of short interest to our trading procedure, we see that it is not a minus factor in the consideration of an upside breakout like the other factors mentioned above. A large relative short position is, however, a very distinct minus factor when the trader is considering the establishment of a short position on the strength of a downside breakout. It is here that an important error may be committed. The combination of a "thin stock" (small floating supply) with a high short position is one that can be fatal to the short-seller, regardless of an overwhelming number of plus factors for the validity of the breakout.

Just how large the short interest must be to constitute a real danger is a difficult question to answer. A good rule-of-thumb is that a short interest in excess of 5 per cent of the total shares outstanding can be considered to have some definite effects upon the price movements of the stock. If further investigation uncovers a floating supply much smaller than the shares outstanding, the price effect can be substantial. A good rule for our trading system is to decide beforehand that whenever a short position is being considered and the short interest approaches 5 per cent, then a thorough investigation will be made into the floating supply and the average daily trading volume. If it is found that the floating supply is considerably less than the total supply outstanding, the position will be abandoned, or at least a very close stop will be maintained. In any case, the greater the short interest beyond the 5 per cent mark, the more potential danger in the short sale.

Finally, it must be remembered that the short interest has a *potential* effect and may not always necessarily affect the trading prices significantly. Often, the short interest may be liquidated slowly over a period of time or may represent an "arbitrage" position. The danger to the chartist is the potential of the explosive "short squeeze," as short-sellers are frightened out by sudden bullish news or sharp rallies. The high short interest is potential fuel to any rally and a potential cushion to any decline. It must be definitely considered a bullish factor, and thus a detriment to the short seller.

ANTICIPATING THE BREAKOUT

Before leaving the breakout, there is another important consideration. A great temptation to any chartist is to anticipate the breakout from an attractive pattern. Because the pattern is attractive, it is difficult to give up the few additional points to be sure. This is especially true when the pattern is quite large and waiting means giving up substantial profit. Does this problem exist in our integrated system?

In general, the strict charting principle of not anticipating breakouts should be followed. In our system, however, there are a number of situations where it may be done under carefully controlled conditions. Before explaining, we may be able to eliminate a few situations from the outset. First, there should be no anticipation until the chartist is experienced. Second, the small patterns where the price objective is small should be eliminated. The amount of money saved is small and when compared with the small potential profit, it makes the anticipation seem hardly worthwhile in view of the added risk. Third, since the short sale is inherently more dangerous, anticipation should be ruled out.

Now, let's look at the conditions under which anticipation may be used to increase the potential profit. The first rule should be obvious; if the pattern is large, well-formed, and a harbinger of a large move and, in addition, meets most of the other qualifications mentioned in our checklist, a position may be taken before the breakout. The second rule, actually a part of the first, is that the fundamentals should be out-standing if the trader is going to gamble on the technical by anticipating the breakout. The breakout should never be anti-cipated if the fundamentals are questionable or weak. Proba-bly the most helpful technical tool to be used in anticipating a breakout is the group chart analysis mentioned earlier. If the stock under observation has not quite broken out, but several other stocks in the industry have already formed and completed similar patterns, a position is warranted prema-turely. Finally, although stop orders are always a helpful tool, they are a necessity in this instance. A position taken prior to the breakout should always be protected with a close stop order. In fact, it may be made a condition that such a position will not be taken unless the chartist can pinpoint a well-defined spot for his protective stop order beforehand.

Although the rules above can certainly help to lessen the danger inherent in the premature technical position, it must be remembered that such a position entails more risk than one which is taken *after* the breakout. There is another rea-son, however, that I favor an early position in an outstand-ingly bullish pattern where the fundamentals are also good. Very often, the bullish pattern that fails is still bullish. It is usually a signal that the technical position is growing stronger, even though it was not strong enough to complete the pattern this time. If the fundamentals are also good, the trader may, at his option, maintain his position and still profit. This is a good point to remember on all breakouts. The breakouts that fail to follow through can give the trader as much useful information as the successful pattern. Very often, these unsuccessful patterns are merely harbingers of good things to come, or in the case of the bearish pattern, of lower prices ahead. The bearish pattern that actually has enough power to breakout (which usually means that a signif-icant support point is penetrated) is still a bearish technical occurrence, even if there is no follow through to the break-out. It remains as a warning that the technical picture is deteriorating. The bullish pattern that fails has similar implications. Wise placements of stop orders or a firm convic-tion in the fundamental strength of the stock can often help the trader to maintain his position even though the original breakout failed to perform as expected. This, of course, is one of the advantages of mixing together all available tools.

As a final note to the anticipation of breakouts, there is a common technique that is quite helpful. If the conditions are right for a position prior to the actual breakout, the trader may take a position with half of the usual number of shares that he ordinarily trades before the breakout. If the breakout then occurs, he may add the other half to his position. In this way, he eliminates half of the risk and saves half of the money he would lose by waiting for the breakout.

SUMMARY

This chapter, first of all, is intended more for the trader who is ready and willing to place an increased emphasis upon the technical side of the trading system that we have been building. He is ready to take the final step of selecting his trades on a chart basis rather than from the pre-selected list of strong fundamental stocks suggested in the intermediate stage of our system. It is presumed that he has already made considerable progress in learning the technical approach. The material introduced in this chapter is meant as a further refinement of the technical approach, which is helpful even if the reader decides to continue to select his trades only from the approved list on the basis of fundamental analysis.

The most important need for this discussion is that the breakout area is most crucial to the chart trader and is the area where most mistakes are made. As mentioned earlier, the greatest fault of the new chartist is that he becomes too enamoured with the semblance of science in charting. He automatically follows even the pattern that only vaguely resembles a valid pattern. His lack of selectivity soon leads to discouragement and failure because he expects too much of charting. To avoid this early discouragement, the chartist should follow only those patterns that are almost sure to work. How is this done? It is easier than it sounds. The chartist needs only to make fewer trades and be willing to be idle at times until the pattern appears that meets all of the qualifications. The greatest advantage to our system is that we stand willing to use any helpful tool and are not hampered by tying ourselves to one camp or the other. In this way we can eliminate as much risk as possible by insisting upon as many qualifications as possible, both of a fundamental as well as of a technical nature. That is what this chapter has tried to do; to remove as much risk as possible at the critical point . . . the breakout.

Chapter 14

THE FINISHING TOUCHES

There is still a very good chance that you may master the technical approach, the fundamental approach, the successful blending of the two and still fail as a short-term trader. There is still a final ingredient that every successful trader has, which is very difficult to define. It might be called the proper trading temperament or trading psychology. The important traits may be objectivity, courage or, at times, the unbeatable combination of ignorance and confidence. It is here that many intelligent and knowledgeable traders are beaten. I am reminded here of the many people that I have met with systems to beat the horses that work well on paper but fall apart once they go to the track. They either lose confidence or courage at important points. The best laid plans in the stock market may also go astray for the same reasons.

There are, doubtless, many to whom the important traits for trading come naturally and who only lack the proper training. There are also some who, no matter how skillful they become, will never master completely these same ingredients. For most, however, the important skills can be mastered and the relevant psychological traits improved.

In this final chapter we will attempt to lay out some of the important pitfalls that the beginning trader may encounter. They are, for the most part, separate from any technical or fundamental skills that we have learned up to this point. Unless they are recognized and avoided, much of the skill learned up to this point is only partially effective. Once they are considered and the advice given incorporated into our already broad approach, you should be totally prepared to trade successfully.

1. HAVE A SYSTEM AND STICK TO IT

This is very common and very good advice to most traders. The trader should always be operating within some broad and organized framework. We have tried to do this for the short-

188

term trader, with our system combining the technical and fundamental approaches. Though the system may be well organized, there are still a number of potential trouble spots.

One problem that many chartists have in common is the failure to be perfectly objective in reading their charts. They will be adept at spying and acting upon signals to take a new position, but they seem to have a blind spot when signals are given to liquidate their positions. The problem is not too acute when there is a profit involved when the liquidation signal is given. But when a loss is involved, the blind spot seems the worst. One problem is, of course, the reluctance to admit an error and to take a loss. More important, the trader is not being honest with himself and certainly not objective. Though he might have stressed the technical strength of the stock when he took the position, he suddenly decides to ignore the technical deterioration of the stock and, instead, begins to build a fundamental case for staying with his position. In our previous chapters, it was intimated that a position could be held by the short-term trader for the long term if the fundamentals warrant it, but if the fundamental analysis is done after the fact, there is a serious question of how objective the trader is.

2. DON'T TRADE WITH THE BREAD MONEY

This is an excellent piece of advice, aimed particularly at aiding the trader to remain objective at all times. It is very difficult to remain objective when the funds used to trade with are extremely important to the everyday well-being of the trader. For this reason, the only funds used for trading purposes should be those that are truly "extra," and their loss would not mean an immediate decline in the standard of living of the trader.

Even with speculative money, moreover, it is good advice for the beginner to work into trading slowly, committing only a part of his funds at a time. Above all, don't trade with money that you have temporarily. There are several reasons why this makes the chances even slimmer. First, the problem of objectivity is still important. Second, you will find yourself becoming more and more impatient with your trades. Finally, it always seems that just at the time you need the funds for other reasons, the market price of your trades will be at the most disadvantageous.

3. OVER-ENTHUSIASM

There is certainly nothing wrong with an enthusiastic trader, but when he goes overboard, he is in trouble. Such is often the situation in short-term trading. Frequently, a trader will become very enthusiastic about a trade and increase his position to try to make the most of it. When he is wrong, the resulting loss is quite large.

There is nothing wrong with adding to a position if it is done logically and objectively. There is a right way and a wrong way to "pyramid" or "average up." Once a good basic position has been taken in a stock, additional purchases should be made in increasingly smaller amounts, and only when the chart has given additional confirming signals that the trend is still intact or additional favorable fundamentals have come to light. The position should look like Pyramid A below. Some traders, however, like to take a small initial position and then round out their basic position. Their position would look more like Pyramid B.

X	X	XXXXX
XX	XX	XXXX
XXX	XXX	XXX
XXXX	XXXX	XX
XXXXX	XXXXX	X
	XX	
A	*B*	*C*

Unfortunately, many traders get carried away in their enthusiasm and do just the opposite. They are a little unsure at first but then begin to add to their rising stock at increasingly higher prices, in increasingly larger amounts and at no meaningful intervals save their sudden spurts of enthusiasm. The result is a pyramid like that in Pyramid C above. The average price of their total position is very near the current market price, so that a minor decline will suddenly turn their early paper profits into an overall losing position. Instead of

190

remaining very objective, with a fine cushion of profit and oblivious to minor fluctuations, every slight selling spree will have him ready to run for cover. We learned from our earlier chapters that the chartist must always be willing to give up a few points to be sure the trend is turning. Certainly, the trader has made it difficult for himself on this point with his overextended position.

A different type of overenthusiasm is the situation in which the trader takes a technical position in a stock but gradually becomes overenthusiastic about the long-term outlook for the stock simply because it is going in the right direction for him. He makes the mistake of setting some drastically higher price objective, not through chart analysis nor through fundamental analysis, but simply through his enthusiasm. He begins to believe this price prediction so strongly that he loses all objectivity in his chart analysis, and refuses to believe the trend will turn before his objective is reached. Later, after he has missed several signals to liquidate the position and the price has gone against him by a considerable amount, he finally decides that the long-term potential of the stock is not so attractive as he thought previously. I'm sure the reader has heard this story in one form or another many times.

4. IMPATIENCE

Impatience is another trait that ruins many of the best-laid plans. It takes two forms: First, the trader who cannot stay on the sidelines and must have *all* of his money committed *all* of the time. He must, by necessity, cheat on his checklist and accept many borderline trades, rather than wait for those that seem surer for success.

Another manifestation of this trait appears in the trader who jumps from one trade to another, often accepting very small profits. His excuse is that alternative trades looked better. In his eagerness to find the stock that will take the biggest price move he, paradoxically, ends up not staying in any stock long enough to take advantage of any large move even when he selects the right ones. He should, instead, see each trade through to its end . . . i.e., until the trend is reversed.

5. DIVERSIFY YOUR TRADES

This is good advice for the beginning chartist for several reasons. First, by spreading the trading funds among several trades, there is an opportunity to learn faster through experiencing more different situations. Second, he guards against one crippling error that can deplete his trading fund until he becomes more adept. Finally, it can help to cure the impatience mentioned above by enabling the trader to hold more positions. He may not feel badly at missing a trade if he can, at least, have a small position in the stock.

All too often the average trader is looking for the "big kill" and puts his money in one stock. Not only does this tend to make him more impatient but he also becomes less objective. He will tend to take a profit too quickly, since he has more at stake, and he will also tend toward overenthusiasm and blindness to bad news. He will also tend to wait too long before taking a loss when he does decide he is wrong because, chances are, the loss will be a large one. When his money is spread among several trades, he can not only follow good charting principles and take losses when they should be taken but they will tend to be a smaller proportion of his entire trading fund. It is difficult to give up enough points to be sure of a reversal in trend when there is a large position.

6. CUT LOSSES SHORT AND LET YOUR PROFITS RUN

We certainly cannot leave this chapter without repeating this old saw. It is almost as well known as "Buy Low and Sell High" and not too much more helpful in itself. It is certainly sound trading advice but for most it is easier said then done. It is hoped, however, that this book has given you enough tools to make it a reality.

With the use of charts, the trader should assess the potential profit and loss of every trade before a position is taken. The potential profit should always be much larger than any potential loss. The situation where the stock could conceivably go in either direction in equal magnitudes should be avoided. We have also seen how charts can be used effectively in placing stop loss orders. With a logical spot to place his stop, the trader can decide on his maximum loss before taking his position. We have also seen how a trailing stop order can be used to follow the trend and allow the greatest profit possible.

7. DON'T REVERSE POSITIONS

In most trading situations it is not a good tactic to immediately take the opposite position when a stock has been liquidated. As we have seen from charting, there is not usually one magic moment when a trend is reversed. It is usually better procedure to liquidate the position on one chart signal, but then to await another confirming signal to take the opposite side of the market. This is especially good advice when the trade that was liquidated was a loss. Too often the anger at taking a loss results in a feeling of "getting even" with the stock by trying to make the money back in the same stock. Waiting for a confirming signal also allows a "cooling-off period." It may even be better always to move to a different stock whenever a loss is taken specifically to avoid this feeling, which most often causes the trader to lose his objectivity. Finally, when the position is immediately reversed, unless the entire market reversed itself, the trader will find himself on the wrong side of the market, assuming he was trading with the trend in the first place.

8. DOUBLE UP ON LOW-PRICED STOCKS

After trading for some time, most traders will tend to fall into a pattern as to how much of their funds they will tie up in any single trade. If, for example, they are trading in a $40 to $50 stock, they will buy a round lot of 100 shares. Once this dollar amount of $4000 to $5000 is settled upon, it should also apply to low-priced stocks. That is, instead of also buying a round lot of say, $10 stock, a position of 400 shares should be taken.

There is a very important reason for this advice. The trader may be perfectly willing to settle for a 20 per cent profit, for example, in his $40 stock because in absolute amounts it is a respectable profit of $800. This same trader would probably not be satisfied with a 20 per cent profit on a round lot of a $10 stock because the absolute amount of $200 less commissions and other expenses does not seem worthwhile. It is always necessary to consider *percentage* gains in trading. The upshot of this is that, unless this advice is followed, most traders will have the tendency to *overstay* the market when trading in low-priced stocks, looking for similar absolute profits to those from higher-priced stocks.

9. KEEP YOUR TRADING TO YOURSELF

There are many reasons for this very sage advice, not all of which are relevant to this book. There are, however, a few good reasons that will have an effect on your trading results. First, the trader should constantly strive to think for himself. Many a good trade is missed because, after conducting a good analysis and concluding that a position should be taken, a trader decides not to go ahead because of some chance remark made by someone who probably knows much less about the particular stock. *Don't take anyone's counsel but your own when taking a position unless he gives you some important information that you missed in your analysis.* If you have done a good analysis this would not usually be the case, so the best procedure is to talk to no one. Another equally important reason for avoiding such talk is that it adds further complicating emotions into your trading. Once others know of your trade positions you will often be afraid to sell out at a loss when you should because you are afraid of "losing face" with your boardroom friends. Likewise, you may be afraid of taking a premature profit.

10. DON'T TRADE AGAINST THE TREND

There is an extremely widespread tendency on the part of most traders to trade always from the long side of the market. This is fine as long as the market is rising, for the odds are with them. They must, however, learn how to stay on the sidelines when the market is falling or learn how to trade the short side in these situations. Unfortunately, most traders continue to trade from the long side even when they know the market is in a downtrend. They hope to pick out those limited number of stocks that will fight the trend. The odds are now, of course, against them, and they tend to lose many of the profits they accumulated during the upswing in the market. When the market is rising, trade only from the long side. When the market is falling, trade only from the short side or stay on the sidelines.

Another variation to this problem is the trader who, while he knows the trend of a particular stock is up, attempts also to take advantage of the short-term declines within the uptrend by shorting for a few quick points. The trader who practices this dangerous game is on the wrong side of the market half of the time, which makes little sense.

11. AVERAGE DOWN ONLY WHEN THE TREND HAS TURNED

Anyone who has mastered the art of chart trading should not fall into the trap of buying more stock merely because it has fallen a few points from the high. I'm sure the road is strewn with the bones of many a bargain hunter who found out that there were even better bargains later. If a trader feels compelled to average down on his position, it should be done only when the trend has definitely turned on the charts.

12. DON'T LIQUIDATE BECAUSE YOU HAVE A PROFIT

Just as a position should never be taken in a stock without several very good reasons, a stock should never be sold without a very good reason. It is not a good reason to liquidate merely because a profit exists. Liquidate only when there is good reason to believe that the trend is reversing, regardless of how large the profit. This type of thinking is obviously necessary, if the trader hopes to put some teeth into the trading principle of cutting losses short while letting profits run.

13. ACT PROMPTLY

Don't vacillate. The only way that you will find out if you are a good trader is to follow your conclusions promptly. If you decide a stock should be sold, sell it immediately. Don't put it off or ask other's advice. All too often, traders become "married" to their stocks. All their analysis may point to liquidation but they instead just hold on because they are used to holding the stock. As well as having a good reason to buy or sell, the trader should always have a good reason to hold.

A FINAL WORD

There are doubtless a great number of additional procedural and psychological pitfalls made by many traders. Those listed here have been some of the most widespread. The important point is that the trader should be constantly analyzing not only stocks, but also his behavior, to see if he is developing bad habits in his trading. Once you have developed this introspection and added it to the well-organized system outlined in this book, consistent trading profits should be assured. Good Luck.